TRANSNATIONAL BUSINESS AND CORPORATE CULTURE

PROBLEMS AND OPPORTUNITIES

edited by

STUART BRUCHEY
ALLAN NEVINS PROFESSOR EMERITUS
COLUMBIA UNIVERSITY

T0358435

THE ECONOMIC IMPACT OF TRANSBORDER TRUCKING REGULATIONS

JOHN T. JONES

Routledge
Taylor & Francis Group

NEW YORK AND LONDON

First published 1999 by Garland Publishing, Inc.

This edition published 2013 by Routledge
711 Third Avenue, New York, NY 10017, USA
2 Park Square, Milton Park, Abingdon, Oxfordshire OX14 4RN

First issued in paperback 2016

Routledge is an imprint of the Taylor and Francis Group, an informa business

Copyright © 1999 John T. Jones
All rights reserved

Library of Congress Cataloging-in-Publication Data

Jones, John T. (John Travis)
    The economic impact of transborder trucking regulations /
John T. Jones.
        p.   cm. — (Transnational business and corporate cul-
ture)
    Includes bibliographical references and index.
    ISBN 0-8153-3252-1 (alk. paper)
    1. Trucking—United States. 2. Trucking—Law and legisla-
tion—Economic aspects—United States. 3. Trucking—North
America. I. Title. II. Series.
HF5623.J66 1998
388.324'0973—dc21
                                                                        98-45172

ISBN 13: 978-1-138-96825-7 (pbk)
ISBN 13: 978-0-8153-3252-7 (hbk)

To Patti

Contents

Tables and Figures

Foreword

Trade barriers impede the free flow of commodities across international borders. In both Europe and North America, trade barriers are coming down. Border crossing points in Europe used to be thriving commercial centers, catering to truckers who had to endure long delays for inspections and paperwork. With the opening of trade under the European Union, many of these same places are now ghost towns, with trucks whizzing past international border crossings much like trucks in the United States move from one state to another. The removal of impediments to transporting goods across borders in Europe clearly reduces costs of goods sold and results in a social gain.

The North American Free Trade Agreement contains provisions that ultimately will enable trucks to move just as freely between Mexico, Canada, and the United States. John Jones has undertaken a study of the effects of trade restrictions on the transportation of goods by truck between the United States and Canada and Mexico. He has found that prior to NAFTA, transborder trucking was much less restricted between the U.S. and Canada than between the U.S. and Mexico. As a result, roughly twice as many resources per dollar of traded goods have been devoted to local trucking and courier services, warehousing and storage, and transportation brokering services at the Mexican border as at the Canadian border. These are resources that can be transferred to other uses as NAFTA takes full effect.

Jones' book provides a thorough investigation of the trucking industry in North America. He reviews the history of motor carrier regulations, especially the regulations affecting transborder trucking. The current structure of the trucking industry is carefully described. Much institutional detail is included about similarities and differences between hauling goods across the Canadian and Mexican borders, as well as a thorough discussion of the economics of within country and transborder trucking. Toward that end, Jones collects data and analyzes the effects of different regulatory regimes on the optimal load size that truckers choose to haul. He finds that regulations forcing interlining of transborder shipments at the border increase the fixed costs of transborder trucking. When entry barriers are asymmetrically relaxed and foreign truckers are allowed to cross the border into the U.S. but U.S. truckers are prohibited from crossing the border, foreign truckers decrease their fronthaul loads into the U.S. This occurs because foreign truckers perceive a higher probability of full backhaul loads.

Jones goes on to explore the resource cost to the U.S. economy of regulations restricting movement of freight across the U.S.-Mexican and U.S.-Canadian borders. He measures the size of the sectors providing transportation arrangement services, transportation services, and warehousing services, and estimates econometrically how these sectors have changed as regulations affecting transborder trucking have changed. In this way he is able to estimate the dollar value of the resources that have been diverted from other uses to serving the transborder trucking sector.

All in all, John Jones provides an informative and thought-provoking study of international trucking on the North American continent. Those who want to understand the institutions of trucking will find a thorough discussion. Those who want to understand the history of U.S. trucking regulation, both domestic and international, will learn from Jones' review of the last several decades. Those who want to understand the economic behavior of trucking and other firms in different regulatory environments will find a careful analysis of the industry at both the Mexican and Canadian borders. And finally, those who want to understand where the transborder trucking industry is headed under the deregulation of NAFTA will find the entire book very helpful.

Frank A. Scott, Jr.
Professor of Economics
University of Kentucky

Acknowledgments

I am grateful to several individuals who have contributed to the development of this book, not the least of which is Professor Frank Scott from the University of Kentucky. Frank Scott is singularly responsible for sparking my interest in the trucking industry. His knowledge of regulatory economics along with his excellent suggestions, guidance, and thorough review of the material in this book is greatly appreciated.

I would like to thank Professors Dan Black, John Garen from the University of Kentucky, Mike Webb of Xavier University, and Scott Takacs from Georgetown College for their review and helpful comments on earlier drafts of this material. I would like to acknowledge Professor Richard Beilock from the University of Florida for his guidance on relevant issues concerning international trucking. I would like to thank the participants of the University of Kentucky's Microeconomics Workshop for their constructive comments and suggestions.

Furthermore, I would like to thank John Peele of the Department of Customs for his assistance in acquiring the data used in this book; Chet Estes of ABF Freight and Jerry Derr of Averitt Expression for generously giving their time and information during our frequent interviews. I would like to thank Linda Darr of the American Trucking Association for passing along unpublished material dealing with international trucking which increased my awareness of the finer points of NAFTA.

Last but not least, I would like to thank the administration of Georgetown College for their cooperation in allowing me the time to complete this book.

The Economic Impact
of Transborder Trucking
Regulations

CHAPTER 1

Introduction

Within a relatively short period of time, the trucking industry has evolved from a quasi-competitive structure to one of a complex system of sophisticated networks fraught with diverse competition. Truckers compete directly, and in many instances cooperate, with railroads and the airline industries in the transportation of freight. In the early 1920's trucking firms were small mom-and-pop organizations. Today, many trucking firms operate thousands of trucks and have annual earnings measured in billions of dollars. Technological advances, undreamed of in the past, such as satellite tracking systems, are common in today's world of interstate trucking.

The U.S. domestic trucking industry was once viewed by government officials as an industry with competition so fierce that it was considered destructive and that federal regulations were needed to correct this perceived market imperfection. As such, the U.S. domestic trucking industry was one of the most heavily regulated. Now, still viewed as highly competitive but less than destructive, the U.S. interstate trucking industry is practically free of federal regulations. Ironically, transborder movements of goods by truck are still heavily regulated.

Trade between the U.S. and its contiguous neighbors, Canada and Mexico, is transported mainly by trucks. Based on cargo value, approximately eighty percent of U.S.-Mexican trade (Maltz, Giermanski, and Molina 1996, 8), and an estimated seventy percent of U.S.-Canadian trade (Department of Transportation 1994, 16) is transported by truck. With increased emphasis on free trade, attention is quickly focusing on international trucking. In the days of heavily regulated domestic movements, transborder trucking, trucking across international boundaries, had been only a minor concern of Congress. Since the beginning of federal trucking regulations in 1935, transborder trucking regulations were subsumed in domestic policies. With deregulation in 1980, debate over transborder trucking policy has intensified and has become the centerpiece in discussions of international freight transportation.

Prior to 1980, barriers to entry took the form of transborder regulations at the northern and southern borders of the U.S. The regulations restricted foreign trucks from transporting goods into the U.S. Since 1980, the northern and southern borders have followed divergent paths concerning truck entry policies. After 1987, the U.S.-Canadian border has maintained minimal truck entry regulations. Truckers from the U.S. or Canada need only to satisfy safety standards in order to transport freight across the U.S.-Canadian border. At the present time, transborder trucking is heavily regulated between the U.S. and Mexico.[1] U.S. laws prohibit Mexican motor carriers from transporting goods inside the United States. Mexican motor carrier movements are limited to commercial zones along the international border. The commercial zones are allowed by the Surface Transportation Board, an agency that replaced the Interstate Commerce Commission in 1995 (Spychalski 1997), to facilitate the exchange of trailers and cargo between Mexican and U.S. truckers. A Mexican trucker carrying imports into the U.S. must stop within the zones and exchange cargo with a U.S. carrier, which then transports the cargo the remainder of the trip through the United States. Mexican local laws prohibit U.S. trucks from entering Mexico. As a result, U.S. exports to Mexico must also be interlined at the border within the U.S. commercial zones.

The divergent path of truck entry regulations would have converged with recent negotiations for free trade. The recently signed North American Free Trade Agreement (NAFTA) explicitly addresses the issue of transborder truck entry and harmonizes entry regulations. Under NAFTA, after a seven-year period, transborder trucking between the U.S. and its contiguous neighbors would have been essentially free of entry barriers. Mexican truckers would have been allowed to transport goods directly into the U.S., and U.S. truckers would have been able to do the same in Mexico. The laws already in place that prevent foreign truckers from conducting domestic transport in the U.S. (cabotage) will remain in place. Foreign truckers entering the U.S. will be prohibited from transporting goods domestically in the U.S., and U.S. truckers will be prohibited from transporting goods domestically within the neighboring countries (Schulz 1993, 28). Despite signing NAFTA, the truck entry component of the agreement has been delayed indefinitely by the U.S.

Given the attention deregulating transborder trucking has received from Congress over the years, little has been written in the economics literature on the issue (Pustay 1989, 252). One possible reason for this apparent void is the general lack of data on transborder movements of goods by truck. In this book, data from various government sources will be used to design a panel data set to econometrically measure the effects that past transborder regulations have had on the trucking industry. The results of this study will provide policymakers information for further negotiations and implementation of trade agreements, such as NAFTA. It will also fill a void in the economic literature by providing econometric estimates of the effects of transborder trucking regulations.

Looking at the U.S.-Mexican and U.S.-Canadian borders and the number of trucking related establishments that locate there may provide information to the effect of transborder trucking regulations. Comparing the number of establishments under the SIC 421 (local trucking and courier services), 422 (warehousing and storage), and 473 (transportation services) between the U.S.-Mexican and the U.S.-Canadian borders reveals some interesting results. The U.S.-Mexican border (a more regulated environment) has more establishments for the transference of cargo per dollar of trade than the U.S.-Canadian border (a less regulated environment). Over time, as regulations fell so did the number of establishments located along the border. This provides evidence that resources are being allocated away from productive means toward the borders during periods of increased regulations.

Table 1-1 below compiles the totals and totals adjusted for trade (real dollar value of imports and exports) for the number of establishments within the commercial zones around the land ports of entry along the two borders. To obtain these totals the size of the commercial zones around each port of entry was first estimated. The total number of establishments under SIC 421, 422, and 473 located within the counties that most closely approximates the commercial zones were summed for each border and their totals reported in Table 1-1.

Table 1-1: Total and Total Adjusted for Trade of the Number of Establishments along the U.S.-Mexican and the U.S.-Canadian Borders

	SIC[a]	Total Number of Establishments		Rate of Change	Total Number of Establishments per Trade ($100 million)		Rate of Change
		1977	1991		1977	1991	
U.S.- Mexico Border	421	730	1338	83.29	5.36	2.93	-45.33
	422	83	260	213.25	.61	.57	-6.56
	473	227	524	130.84	1.67	1.15	-31.14
U.S.- Canada Border	421	1,664	2,108	26.69	2.09	1.68	-19.62
	422	105	187	78.10	.13	.14	7.69
	473	126	263	108.73	.15	.22	47.0

Source: Department of Commerce. Economics and Statistics Administration. 1977 and 1991. *County Business Patterns*.
[a]SIC 421 denotes Local Trucking and Courier Service; SIC 422 denotes Public Warehousing and Storage; SIC 473 denotes Arrangement for Transportation of Freight and Cargo.

The table contains the universe of establishments under SIC 421, 422, and 473 located within the commercial zones around each land port of entry along both borders for the years 1997 and 1991.

The U.S.-Canadian border has more establishments under SIC 421 (Local Trucking and Courier Services) than the U.S.-Mexican border for the years 1977 and 1991. The U.S.-Canadian border had a total of 1,664 establishments for the year 1977, and 2,108 establishments for the year 1991. The U.S.-Mexican border had only 730 establishments in 1977, and 1,338 establishments in 1991. However, the U.S.-Mexican border had more establishments under SIC 473—Arrangement for Transportation for Freight and Cargo than the U.S.-Canadian border. For the years of 1977, the U.S.-Mexican border had 227 establishments, and in 1991 the U.S.-Mexican border had 524 establishments. The U.S.-Canadian border had only 126 establishments in 1977, and 263 establishments in 1991. In 1977, the U.S.-Canadian border had more establishments under SIC 422 (Public Warehousing and Storage) with 105 establishments compared to 83 establishments along the U.S.-Mexican border. This was reversed in 1991. The U.S.- Mexican border had more establishments in public warehousing and storage in 1991 with 260 establishments, compared to the U.S.-Canadian border with 187 establishments.

Comparing the rate of change in the number of establishments along both borders from the year 1977 to the year 1991 reveals that the U.S.- Mexican border has experienced the greatest rate of increase for all three types of establishments. The rate of increase ranges from a low of 83.29 percent, for trucking and courier service establishments, to a high of 213.25 percent for public warehousing and storage establishments (the rate of increase for establishments that arrange for transportation for freight and cargo, SIC 473, is 130.84 percent). The U.S.-Canadian border shows a rate of increase ranging from 26.69 percent for local trucking and courier service establishments to 108.73 percent for establishments that arrange for the transportation for freight and cargo (public warehousing and storage establishments shows a rate of increase of 78.1 percent). These changes were occurring during the period in time when regulations were increasing along the U.S.-Mexican border, and the U.S.-Canadian border was under going deregulation. The changes in the number of establishments along the U.S.-Mexican and the U.S.-Canadian borders may merely be reflecting a greater need for border agents due to increases in the volume of trade, and not due to the change in regulations. In order to get a clearer picture, the number of establishments need to be adjusted for the volume of trade.

To adjust the total number of establishments for the real dollar value of trade, current dollar values of imports and exports (measured in millions of dollars) were added together for the U.S.- Mexican border and also for the U.S.-Canadian border for the year 1977 and again for the year 1991. The summed values give the total nominal dollar value of trade crossing each border for each year. The real dollar value of trade was obtained by deflating the nominal dollar value of trade by the U.S. GDP deflator index. The deflated numbers give the real dollar value of trade in one hundred million dollar units. Then, since approximately 80 percent of all international trade between the U.S., Mexico, and Canada is carried by trucks, the real dollar value of trade was multiplied by 0.8 to get an approximate real dollar value of trade carried by trucks. The total number of establishments in each category were divided by this number to get the total number of establishments adjusted for trade.

When the establishments are adjusted for trade, the U.S.-Mexican border shows the greatest number of establishments for all three categories. In 1977, there were 5.36 establishments for local trucking and courier services for every one hundred million dollars of trade crossing the U.S.-Mexican border. Along the U.S.-Canadian border, there were 2.09 establishments for local trucking and courier services needed for the same volume of trade for the same year. For each one hundred million dollars of trade, there were 0.61 warehousing and storage establishments located along the U.S.-Mexican border in 1977. The U.S.- Canadian border shows 0.13 establishments in warehousing and storage for the same time period and the same level of trade. Most striking of all the results is the difference in the number of establishments for arranging transportation for freight and cargo. Along the U.S.-Mexican border there were 1.67 establishments per one hundred million dollars of trade in 1977. Along the U.S.-Canadian border there were 0.15 establishments for the same level of trade in 1977. These results suggest that transborder trucking across the US.-Mexican border requires more border agents to facilitate the transference of goods than was needed along the U.S.-Canadian border in 1977.

Comparing the number of establishments per dollar of trade along the U.S.-Mexican border from 1977 to 1991 shows that the number of establishments in all three categories have decreased. Though the U.S.-Mexican border shows a decrease, the number of establishments is still greater than the number of establishments along the U.S.-Canadian border in 1991. The rate of decrease ranges from a low of 6.56 percent for warehousing and storage, to a high of 45.33 percent for local trucking and courier services (establishments in the arrangement for transportation for freight and cargo decreased at a 31.14 percent rate). This decrease in all categories of establishments along the U.S.-Mexican border may be explained best by the easing of tension between the U.S. and Mexico and by gains in efficiency from innovations in transborder trucking technology. Mexico has recently reduced the barriers on foreign truck entry. In 1990, Mexico's former president, Carlos Salinas de Gortari, took steps to clean up Mexican Customs along the U.S.-Mexican border. The Mexican government reduced the power of local unions who controlled the border. The method of "mordida," or bribing local officials to ensure international cargo would pass through Customs unabated, has been eliminated (Bowman 1991, 90). Today, Mexican officials allow, on a limited basis, U.S. carriers access into the Mexican border region to drop off trailers so Mexican truckers can haul the cargo the remaining distance into Mexico (Department of State 1994; Molina and Giermanski 1994, 51). Telecommunications and direct computer linkages between shippers and Custom's officials at the border have reduced the paperwork necessary for transborder shipping and increased the speed in the transference of cargo. These factors are most likely the cause of the reduction in the number of establishments used to facilitate transborder trucking along the U.S.-Mexican border from 1977 to 1991.

In 1977, the U.S.-Canadian border had 2.09 establishments for local trucking and courier services per one hundred million dollars of trade. In 1991, the U.S.-Canadian border had 1.68 establishments per one hundred million dollars of trade. This is a 19.62 percent rate of decline in the number of establishments involved in local trucking and courier services from 1977 to 1991. As seen before, the U.S.-Mexican border shows a larger rate of decline in this type of establishment with a 45.33 percent rate of reduction. The reduction in the number of trucking and courier service establishments along both borders is partially explained by gains in efficiency due to the easing of entry barriers and partially by the Interstate Commerce Commission (ICC) redefining the size of the commercial zones in 1977. The ICC adopted a population and mileage formula to determine the size of commercial zones (Interstate Commerce Commission, 1976). Commercial zones prior to 1977 were defined on an individual basis. The new method of defining the commercial zones increased the size of all previously existing commercial zones. The increased size of the zones also allowed foreign trucks to transport international freight short distances across the U.S. border without government interference. International trucks were permitted to drop off freight on the U.S. side of the border so domestic U.S. trucks could haul the cargo the rest of the distance into the U.S. Prior to this action, local trucking and couriers were needed to dray cargo across the border. Because Mexican and Canadian truckers could transport freight directly into the U.S., these specialized truckers were no longer needed and their numbers were reduced. Also, prior to the Motor Carrier Act (MCA) of 1980, the ICC started to liberalize the interpretation of the requirements for entry into the U.S. interstate trucking industry. More foreign truckers were awarded authority. This allowed the foreign truckers to perform direct-line services to receivers in the U.S. The foreign truckers completely bypassed the local trucking and courier service establishments at the border. The liberalizing of entry regulations by the ICC, and the expansion of the commercial zones together reduced the demand for interlining services, and the number of local trucking and courier service establishments decreased.

Between the years 1977 and 1991, the U.S.-Canadian border experienced a 47 percent increase in the number of establishments for arranging for transportation for freight and cargo. This is a relatively large percentage increase. Investigating this phenomena further, it was found, from 1977 to 1986, the number of establishments per dollar of trade had remained fairly constant at roughly 0.15 brokers per one hundred million dollars of trade. Between the years of 1986 to 1991, the variation in the number of establishments per dollar of trade increased. The higher variation has highs of 0.22 establishments per one hundred million dollars of trade in 1988 and again in 1991. The lows reached a minimum at 0.17 establishments per one hundred million dollars of trade in 1986. The average number of establishments for arranging for transportation for freight and cargo per one hundred million dollars of trade over the years from 1977 to 1986 is 0.153. The average number of establishments per one hundred million dollars of trade for the years 1986 to 1991 is 0.195. The year when the increase appears to have occurred is 1987. The year 1987 is when Canada enacted the Motor Vehicle Transportation Act (MVTA). This Act allowed easier entry into Canada by U.S. carriers. A possible explanation for the greater number of establishments for the arrangement of transportation for freight and cargo at the border after 1987 is an increased demand for services to fill empty backhauls. Canada allowed U.S. trucks to enter their county in 1987, but the MVTA did not affect the ban on cabotage in Canada. Once a U.S. carrier entered Canada to drop off cargo, unless the carrier had prearranged a load coming back to the U.S., the carrier would have to travel empty until safely back in the States. Empty backhauls are costly. Border agents who arrange for the transportation of freight and cargo located along the border could secure a load for the returning truck as soon as it crossed the border. This would reduce the cost of traveling empty the entire trip back into the U.S. The increase demand for the services to fill empty backhauls will be directly related to the cost savings to the truckers. The longer the trip back into the U.S. for the returning trucker the stronger the demand for, and profits to, the firms already at the border performing such services. The increase in profits would attract more transportation brokers to the border, and therefore, increase the number of establishments under SIC 473 along the U.S.-Canadian border.

In all three categories of establishments, the gap between the difference in the number of establishments per dollar of trade between the two borders has narrowed over time. This suggests the number of establishments needed to facilitate transborder trucking across the two borders are moving closer together. The convergence is mostly due to the U.S.-Mexican border's declining number of establishments per dollar of trade. This is occurring because of the easing of transborder regulations between the U.S. and Mexico.

By studying the changes in the number of trucking related establishments along the border, we will be able to measure the impact that transborder truck entry regulations have on the allocation of resources. Comparing the number of border establishments between the two time periods and across the two borders offers insight to the effects of transborder truck entry regulations, but more in-depth analysis is needed.

The next chapter will present a brief history of regulations placed on the U.S. domestic and transborder trucking industries, followed by a discussion of the structure and institutional factors of the U.S. domestic and transborder industries in Chapter 3. In Chapter 4, an empirical study of the changes in the load sizes carried by transborder truckers resulting from various transborder regulations will be presented. Then, in Chapter 5, an investigation of the number of border establishments related to transborder trucking operations and the changes caused by different regulatory regimes will be presented. Finally in Chapter 6, a summary of the results will conclude this study.

NOTE

1. Non-trucking regulations have also intensified in recent years. From its inception in April until November, 1997, the Illegal Immigration Reform and Immigrant Responsibility Act has banned 27,774 people from entering the U.S. for five-year periods. Ninety-one percent were Mexican (De Santis 1998, A13).

CHAPTER 2

History of Motor Carrier Regulations

Regulations placed on the United States motor carrier industry can be traced as far back as the Civil War. Prior to federal regulations, Congress abdicated responsibility of regulating motor carrier movements to the states. Pennsylvania, in 1914, was the first state to regulate trucking (Department of Transportation 1990, 13) followed by Illinois that same year, then Colorado, New York, Maryland, and Wisconsin in 1915, and then California and Utah in 1917 (Teske, Best, and Mintrom 1995, 28). By 1925 thirty-five states regulated freight and passenger carriers (Robyn 1987, 13). Until 1925, the states maintained full responsibility for regulating intra- as well as interstate trucking. The states controlled interstate shipments when a motor carrier's routes passed though their jurisdiction. Eventually the U.S. Supreme Court, called on by the railroads to harmonize state regulations, in the case *Buck v. Kuykendall* in 1925 denied the states the right to regulate interstate movements (Felton and Anderson 1989, 3).

In 1876, the first federal regulatory bill was passed that regulated surface transport. The bill eliminated Philadelphia and Reading Railroads' ability to offer rebates, a form of price discrimination used by the railroads. Members of the fledgling railroad pool, a cartel made up of mostly railroad owners, were strong supporters of the regulatory move. The railroad owners wanted to avoid competition among themselves in order to maintain collusive pricing. The ratified bill eliminated price discrimination and discounting which were means of cheating on collusive agreements (Moore 1972, 6). The railroad pool continued to lobby and push for measures that would strengthen the collusive bonds between the railroads.

In 1887, the Interstate Commerce Act was signed by President Cleveland, and the Interstate Commerce Commission (ICC) was formed. The first Chairman of the Commission, Thomas M. Cooley, was a conservative railroad man. The other commission members were also connected in some form with the railroad industry (Moore 1972, 11-12). The Interstate Commerce Act of 1887, which authorized the existence of the ICC, was designed to stabilize the seemingly chaotic railroad industry (Teske, Best and Mintrom 1995, 25). The Act forbade price discrimination and discounts, as well as geographical discrimination. All of these were problems inhibiting collusion that the railroad pool wanted to eliminate. The Act required railroads to publish their rates which reduced rogue railroads' ability to rapidly change their rates and weaken price competition. Eventually, regulations formed barriers to entry into and exit from the railroad industry by reducing a railroad's ability to abandon unprofitable lines. The apparent goal was to prevent competition between railroads by setting up each railroad as a local monopoly with specific routes that competitors were forbidden to use and to make it prohibitively costly to enter a market. The complete cartelization of the railroad industry was not possible until the enactment of the Transportation Act of 1920. The Transportation Act authorized the ICC to control minimum rates set by railroads (Moore 1972, 22) Controlling minimum rates limited the railroads' ability to undercut the ICC prescribed rates for the rail industry. In essence, the one element that leads to the destruction of cartels—cheating on collusive pricing agreements—was essentially eliminated by the Transportation Act of 1920.

In the early 1900's railroads were the main mode of transporting freight. In 1929, as much as three-quarters of the U.S. intercity freight was carried by railroads and nearly 70 percent was still carried by railroads after World War II (Winston et al. 1990, 1). The start of World War I marked the beginning of the end of the railroads' dominance in the interstate shipping market. The interstate trucking industry was in its infancy at that time. Though many railroads were plagued with financial problems, they were well established in the interstate market. The U.S. involvement in World War I demanded mobilization of resources for the war effort. Railroads, being the dominant mode for transporting people and goods, were drawn away from interstate commerce to transport troops and military equipment in preparation for the war. Businesses had to resort to other means for transporting their goods. The relatively insignificant motor carrier industry took up the slack. While military troops and equipment were shipped by rail, domestic cargo was being transported by truck. The door-to-door service and flexibility that the motor carriers provided was an attractive feature to shippers and receivers (Kahn 1988, 14/II). The longer the war persisted the stronger the motor carriers' foothold on interstate commerce became.

After World War I the railroads, threatened by the foothold made by the motor carriers, lobbied Congress to regulate the motor carrier industry. At that time the Interstate Commerce Commission was a pro-railroad organization. The railroads were confident that any regulation of truck movements would favor the railroad industry. The railroads, who were effective lobbyists at the state level, lobbied the federal government to harmonize state-level regulations involving interstate transport by motor carriers. Their efforts were successful and federal regulation of the interstate trucking industry was instituted in 1925 with the case of *Buck and Bush*. The U.S. Supreme Court decided that states could not restrict "wasteful competition and unnecessary operations" of motor carriers unless the state issued a certificate or a permit to an interstate carrier (Nelson 1936, 464-5).

The lobbying efforts continued into the 1930's. The Great Depression in the United States was in full force. Businesses were struggling to survive. Business failures were common. The railroad industry, already in financial dire straits, found the "cutthroat" competition of the motor carriers eroding their dominance in the interstate transport industry even further. Often trucking firms would charge customers prices below the cost of performing their services in hopes of making up the difference on the return hauls. From 1926 to 1932, the railroads saw their revenue drop from $4.906 billion to $2.485 billion as carload tonnage shrank (Childs 1985, 93). The 1932 revenue drop was unprecedented in railroad history. The railroads' poor performance was the catalyst for the enactment of the Emergency Transportation Act of 1933. In addition to simplifying rules of rate making and eliminating revenue sharing, the Act recommended regulating trucking (Moore 1972, 23-6). The railroads were so weakened by the low rates of the truckers that bankruptcies were prevalent. To advert widespread bankruptcies, the Reconstruction

Finance Corporation (funded by the government) lent railroads over $882 million dollars from 1933 to 1935 (Nelson 1936, 466-7). During the Depression there was excess capacity and an oversupply of transportation services. The Depression-ravaged voting public, seeing the drastic measures that businesses resorted to in order to survive, suspected competition in general as being a contributing factor in the downturn of the economy. The movement toward federal regulation of the trucking industry met with little objection by the public. However, there were strong protests made by shippers who suspected that trucking rates would increase as they did under state regulations, and automobile manufactures protested out of fear that the regulations would lead to a decrease in the demand for trucks (Nelson 1936, 466). Several years after the Depression, the struggling railroads pushed for stronger trucking regulations. The Federal Coordinator of Transportation, Joseph Eastman, an influential regulator and a former member of the ICC, was one of the strongest supporters of regulating the trucking industry[1] (Childs 1985, 119-24). Another staunch supporter of trucking regulations was the Security Owners' Association (a railroad lobbyist group made up of investors, national and state banks, trust companies and life insurance companies). In 1932 the SOA, headed by former president Calvin Coolidge and other members who held interest in the railroad industry, lobbied Congress for stronger trucking regulations (Robyn 1987, 13). The newly formed American Trucking Association (ATA), once opposed to government control in favored of self-regulation, realized the benefits of government protection and pushed for the regulation of the industry. The general trucking industry, suffering under reduced demand and strong rate competition, also supported the move to regulate the industry. On August 9, 1935, by the signature of President Roosevelt, the Motor Carrier Act (MCA) gave the ICC the authority to place the interstate trucking industry under its regulatory control (Nelson 1936, 470). The ICC controlled entry, prices, labor practices, and safety requirements of the truckers. One form of trucking that was exempt from regulations were private carriers. Private carriers made up eighty five percent of the industry, most of which were farmers who owned twenty-six percent of all trucks (Childs 1985, 93). The exempt status is a testament to the strength of the agricultural lobbyists. The regulations were similar to the regulations placed on the railroad industry. The motive of the MCA of 1935 was to stem the tide of destructive competition between motor carriers and the railroad industry. At first the trucking regulations appeared to favor the railroads, but eventually they became a means of protecting the trucking industry. The trucking industry responded to the protective measures quickly and began to expand. The railroad industry continued to lose market share to truckers, but the real threat to the railroads occurred when the interstate highways were built. This gave truckers the ability to effectively compete with railroads for interstate commerce. In the 1940's the legal limit on trailers was twenty-seven feet, but in the 1970's the legal limit had increased to forty-five feet (Robyn 1987, 15). The increasing size of trailer capacity allowed truckers to ship larger loads once reserved for the railroad industry. This exacerbated the erosion of the railroads' dominance.

The Motor Carrier Act of 1935 primarily focused on regulating domestic trucking, but it also applied to foreign trucking. Sections of the MCA (for example section 202C) applied specifically to truckers providing service for foreign or domestic transportation (Nelson 1936, 475-6). The MCA was designed to regulate common carriers.[2] Common carriers are truckers who transport general commodities for a fee. The Motor Carrier Act required all common carriers to apply to the Interstate Commerce Commission for a "certificate of convenience and necessity." The certificate specified the services to be performed and the routes the truckers were allowed to travel (Moore 1972, 27). A "grandfather clause" was allowed for trucking firms established prior to June 1, 1935. Firms existing prior to the signing of the Motor Carrier Act were guaranteed the issuance of the certificates of convenience and necessity for their existing routes. New carriers entering the interstate market or existing carriers increasing the number of routes served were required to obtain a certificate. Certificates were issued to carriers if the ICC found the trucking firm to be fit, willing, and able to perform the service proposed and that their services were required by the present and future public convenience and necessity (Moore 1972, 27-28). The certificate also specified the commodities or classes of commodities a carrier could transport. The certificates also limited the range of the motor carriers' movements by specifying the routes that carriers were allowed to travel. The Act also reserved the right for the ICC to suspend changes in the carriers' rates for up to six months, set maximum or minimum rates, or actually set the rates to be charged if the ICC suspected the rates were unreasonable or unjustly discriminatory. In an attempt to reduce price competition, the ICC reduced the carriers' ability to quickly respond to competitive rate changes by requiring all rate changes to be published and adhered to no sooner than thirty days. Contract carriers (carriers who hold a legal agreement to transport goods for specific clients) were exempt from tariff filings. Contract carriers had to acquire a "permit" in order to enter the industry. The authorization of permits and certificates of convenience and necessity could be refused if the carrier's application was successfully protested by competing carriers with similar authority. Nearly all applications were protested by existing carriers.[3]

Some carriers were exempt from the regulations of the MCA of 1935. These exempt carriers carried over 60 percent of the ton-miles of freight moved by trucks in interstate commerce (Robyn 1987, 19). Private carriers hauling their own goods, motor vehicles owned by railroads or freight forwarders incidental to their own business, local carriage, water carriers, and motor vehicles carrying fish, livestock or agricultural commodities were exempt from regulation. Also exempt were vehicles carrying exclusively newspaper or newsprint and trucks owned and operated by agricultural cooperatives. These exemptions were justified because of the rapid obsolescence of the cargo. Agricultural cooperatives were restricted to allow no more than half of their transportation business to be carried by nonmembers. Because of regulations on other forms of trucking and rail services, many private companies found that forming their own transportation system was more cost effective than relying on the increased rates of the regulated trucking system. Exempt motor carriers' rate flexibility severely eroded the railroads' market share (Khan 1988, 18II-24II). Exempt carriers' primarily transported cargo in one direction. At the final destination, the exempt carriers typically would offer cut-rate prices, easily below rail rates, in order to acquire freight to backhaul. The ICC regulations prohibited railroads from matching the exempt carriers' rates; thus, over the years, railroads continued to lose cargo and market share to exempt carriers.

Freight forwarders fell under the ICC's regulatory control in 1942 with the passing of the Freight Forwarder Act. Freight forwarders are third party associates who consolidate less-than-truckload cargo into truckload shipments. They take complete responsibility for the shipping of the goods but do not specialize in transporting the shipments. The only basis for their regulation was to provide consistency with regulations of other freight modes such as railroads, trucks, and barges

(House 1986, 4). Prior to 1942, railroads would often use freight forwarders as a means of non-price competition. The railroads were offering discounts or supplied freight forwarders with facilities or buildings and railcars free of charge to those who could offer superior service. The ICC suspected freight forwarders of unnecessarily creating unwanted competition between the railroads. The suspicion stemmed from the belief that freight forwarders increased the cost of transporting goods because railroads could easily internalize the process and bypass forwarders altogether. Many of the regulations placed on freight forwarders were similar to the regulations applied to common carriers.

The Reed-Bulwinkle Act of 1948 gave antitrust immunity to motor carriers. The law allowed motor carriers to form rate bureaus to set and publish rates for their members. One of the justifications for the rate bureaus was that the publishing of rates required by the Motor Carrier Act of 1935 was overwhelming for small carriers who lacked the resources to comply with the legal requirements. The passing of the Reed-Bulwinkle Act did not go unchallenged. President Harry Truman attempted to stop the Act by vetoing the bill. In his veto message, President Truman cautioned that "the exercise by private groups of this substantial control over the transportation industry involves serious potential harm to the public . . . Power to control transportation rates is power to influence the competitive success or failure of other business. Legislation furthering the exercise of this power by private groups would clearly be contrary to the public interest" (Department of Transportation 1990, 54). Congress overruled the President's veto and the bill became law.

In 1950, there were clear signs that the railroads were losing their dominance to motor carriers. Several labor strikes and a severe coal strike contributed to the railroads losses. In 1950 the *Wall Street Journal* reported that railroads' freight loads were down 7 percent from the year before (April 6, 1950, p.1). By March 31, 1950 Eastern railroads petitioned the ICC to allow the railroads to lower their rates by 25 percent. The request for the rate cuts, as reported by the *Wall Street Journal*, was in response to the loss of market share and the increasing strength of the motor carriers in the industry (April 22, 1950, p. 3). The Interstate Commerce Commission granted the request, and motor carriers continued to prosper.[4]

Trucking companies' operating certificates often were sold on the open market. The market value of some operating certificates was so high that for some trucking companies their most valuable asset was the certificate. Industrywide, the certificates were worth as much as $10 billion in 1997 dollars, and individual firms paid roughly 15 percent of their expected earnings to acquire the operating rights[5] (Moore 1978, 342). The high market value of these operating rights provides evidence that holders of certificates had superior market power over those that did not have certificates, thus they were able to reap higher profits (Kafoglis 1977, 27-32; Palmer 1988, 61; Pustay 1989, 244). The most valuable certificates were the general commodity, regular route. In 1977 eight trucking firms which held general commodity regular route certificates earned returns greater than two times the average of the Fortune 500 companies (Robyn 1987, 17). The general commodity certificates allowed the truckers to transport small parcels in a networking hub-and-spoke fashion that today is known as the Less-than-Truckload (LTL) industry. The LTL industry is the dominant form of trucking today because of the unique cargo-consolidating networks and door-to-door delivery of small packages that cannot be performed by any means other than trucking.

In the mid 1970's, Congress became disenchanted with the ICC regulations over the trucking industry. With promising examples of trucking deregulation in countries like Australia (Joy 1964), Congress moved to deregulate entry into the U.S. trucking industry. With the support of President Jimmy Carter and influential Congressmen like Senator Edward Kennedy, Congress passed the Motor Carrier Act of 1980.[6] The Act greatly eased entry and exit barriers. Before the MCA of 1980, the burden of establishing proof of public convenience and necessity for authority to transport goods over a specific route was placed on the applicant. The MCA of 1980 shifted the burden from the applicant to the incumbent carriers, who were now required to show that the applicant's operations would be inconsistent with the public's convenience and necessity in order for the applications to be denied. The result of the shifting of the burden was that new applications were seldom denied (Interstate Commerce Commission 1981, 4; Federal Trade Commission 1988, 7). In fact, in 1976, the ICC approved only 69.8 percent of applicants; in 1981, approval increased to 98.6 percent (Wilson and Beilock 1993, 14). Prior to 1980, no motor carrier was authorized to operate in all forty-eight states; by 1985, over 4 thousand carriers had that authority (Delaney 1987, 9). As signs of deregulation became eminent, the market value of operating certificates fell from a four-year industry average of $400 thousand from 1975 to 1978 to $15 thousand by 1981 as entry eroded their value (Moore 1983, 37). In 1990, out of the 12,616 applications for common carrier authority and contract carrier permits only 9 were opposed, but eventually all 9 were granted[7] (Senate 1991, 18).

2.1 REGULATIONS AFFECTING TRANSBORDER TRUCKING

Since the Motor Carrier Act of 1980, Congress has been moving away from protecting U.S. motor carriers from themselves to protecting domestic truckers from foreign trucking. Though the regulations in the Motor Carrier Act of 1935 applied to transborder trucking, the laws primarily focused on domestic trucking. It was not until the Motor Carrier Act of 1980 that significant changes in transborder trucking regulations occurred. Prior to 1980, there were some attempts to weaken the regulations on transborder trucking. Concerning transborder trucking with Mexico, in 1955 Mexico's President Luis Cortines signed an agreement with the United States to allow U.S. trucks to operate within a 20-kilometer zone beyond the Mexican border, but until very recently, the agreement has never been enforced (House 1983, 28). Foreign competition within Mexico is not allowed by Mexican authorities. The general denial of foreign truck operations in Mexico is said to be for reasons of national security. The Mexican authorities require the transportation sector of their country to be solely controlled by Mexican nationals for the necessity of mobilizing troops in case of war. The Mexican government feared foreign competition would infringe on Mexico's military mobility. In Mexico, substantial governing power over trucking regulations is left to the local and state governments. The local governments control the border region of Mexico and restrict U.S. truckers from entering Mexico.[8] U.S. motor carriers were permitted to enter Mexico if they paid "mordida" or substantial bribes to local unions (Bowman 1991, 88). Even after paying bribes to local Custom agents to enter Mexico, U.S. carriers often faced the possibility of having their vehicles impounded with additional payments required in order to retrieve their vehicles and leave Mexico (House 1983, 28). As a result, U.S. carriers seldom crossed the U.S.-Mexican border.

Restricting U.S. motor carriers' access was not unique to Mexico. Canada also maintained entry barriers against U.S. trucks. Motor carrier movements were regulated at the provincial level. It was not until 1954 with the Winner Decision that provisions were made to allow federal control over the interprovincial transportation industry. However, the burden of regulating the industry proved to be too great for the federal government. Laws were passed to allow the provinces to control all motor carrier movements in their jurisdiction (Chow 1991, 146). U.S. truckers had to apply separately to each province for operating authority to transport their shipments into Canada if their movements involved the provinces. Canadians also had to apply for ICC authority to interline with U.S. carriers (Sloss 1970, 357-8). The application process was similar to that in existence in the U.S. prior to 1980. The incumbent Canadian firms could protest the application of a U.S. trucker, and the issuance of the operating authority could be denied. This created barriers to the transborder market, but unlike Mexico, some U.S. truckers were awarded certificates to conduct transborder movements. In an investigation of the U.S.-Canadian trucking industry, Ex Parte No. MC-157, investigators showed that in 1980 in the Less-Than-Truckload (LTL) sector, 13.2 percent of international shipments were single-lined, and in the Truckload (TL) sector, 22.1 percent were single-lined, with the majority of the truck movements originating from the U.S. (House 1983, 145).

The Motor Carrier Act of 1980 reduced entry requirements for all motor carrier operations, which included foreign truck operations. Canadian and Mexican haulers could apply for and were awarded operating authority to transport international cargo into the United States.[9] Cargo coming from Canada or Mexico could be brought into the United States by foreign motor carriers who applied for and were awarded operating authority. The number of authorized foreign carriers increased substantially with little sign of reciprocity from either Canada or Mexico. The liberal U.S. entry requirements along with the strong entry restrictions by Canadians and Mexicans created an imbalance in foreign motor carrier entry policies. The American Trucking Association and other trucking interests demanded action to alleviate the imbalance. On September 20, 1982, President Ronald Reagan signed the Bus Regulatory Reform Act into law. Section 6(g) of this act imposed a two-year moratorium on the issuance of certificates of convenience to carriers domiciled in, owned, or controlled by Mexicans or Canadians (House 1983, 28). This Act confines foreign motor carriers who do not have Interstate Commerce Commission authorization, hauling ICC regulated commodities, to the commercial zones around the ports of entry along either the northern or southern border of the United States. On November 29 1982, after an investigation of the policies involving U.S. truck access into Canada (Ex-Parte No. MC-157), President Reagan completely removed the moratorium on issuance of ICC certificates for Canadian motor carriers (House 1983, 38). Canadian officials successfully convinced U.S. policymakers that deregulation was occurring in Canada and that U.S. truckers would soon have complete reciprocal truck access (Chow 1983, 50). The Canadian provinces maintained strong but weakening control over foreign truck entry until 1987.

Though the moratorium continued to apply to Mexican truckers, not all Mexican motor carriers were affected by the moratorium. The moratorium exempted private carriers, agricultural haulers, haulers of less than 10,000 lbs, and haulers who already had operating authority[10] (House 1983, 39). Because of Mexico's unwavering stand on blocking U.S. motor carriers from entering their country, Congress enacted the Surface Transportation Assistance Act of 1982. This Act made it the responsibility of the Department of Transportation to enforce the law requiring Mexican domiciled carriers to follow stringent safety requirements and to carry evidence of financial responsibility within their cabs. This law only applied to for-hire carriers. Within two years, Congress passed the Motor Carrier Safety Act. Sections 225 and 226 of this Act substantially increased the requirements on Mexican motor carriers entering the U.S. Section 226 of this Act restricted entry of Mexican carriers by requiring the carriers to apply for a "Certificate of Registration" from the ICC. The certificates permitted Mexican truckers to operate within the commercial zones along the border. This policy is still in place today. Acquiring the certificate is based on whether the Mexican carrier has insurance and has fulfilled Department of Transportation safety standards. Both carriers of exempt and non-exempt goods are required to apply for the certificate. Without such a certificate Mexican carriers are denied entry into the U.S. (House 1987, 3-4). This act restricts nearly all Mexican motor carriers transporting in the U.S. to operate within the unregulated areas around each port of entry along the U.S.-Mexican border. The unregulated areas, called commercial zones, range in size based on a population-mileage formula established by the ICC in 1977[11] (Interstate Commerce Commission 1976). The commercial zones range in size from 5 miles to 75 miles from the border. The entry barriers in place for Mexican transborder truckers will be eliminated when Mexican reciprocity is achieved with NAFTA.

In August 1992, there were 4,083 Mexican motor carriers holding certificates of registration. The number of Mexican motor carriers holding broader operating authority remains at four, the same number of certificates of public convenience and necessity issued prior to the moratorium of 1982. No Mexican motor carrier has 48-state authority (Senate 1991, 12; Department of Commerce 1993, 13).

The threat of a moratorium on the issuance of ICC operating authorities for Canadian motor carriers was one of the factors that sent the wheels of deregulation moving in Canada.[12] By 1987, Bill C-19, known as the Motor Vehicle Transportation Act (MVTA), was signed into law. MVTA weakened restrictions on foreign motor carrier entry into Canada. MVTA officially started January 1, 1988, but applications for operating authority in Canada were approved prior to this date (Chow 1995, 13). The Act mirrored the deregulation component in the MCA of 1980. The MVTA established a uniform and nationwide entry test for extra-provincial trucking operations based on fitness. The fit, willing, and able license tests were based on safety and insurance requirements. The onus of proof of public necessity was placed on objectors to prove that the public interest would not be served by any new operator[13] (Chow 1991, 162).

In 1990, President George Bush began negotiations with Mexico's President Carlos Salanis to establish an agreement to allow freer trade between the two nations. Canadian officials soon entered the negotiations which eventually culminated in what is known as the North American Free Trade Agreement (NAFTA). NAFTA is an arrangement between the United States, Canada, and Mexico to reduce most trade barriers between the three countries. NAFTA was signed on December 17, 1992 and approved by Congress in November, 1993. The agreement is designed to reduce, if not completely eliminate, most tariffs as well as non-tariff barriers on goods traded between the U.S., Canada, and Mexico. Unlike the Free Trade Agreement between the U.S. and Canada, there is language in NAFTA that specifically addresses transborder trucking. For three years, starting December 17, 1995, Mexican authorities are to allow U.S. and Canadian motor carriers to make pick-up or delivery of international cargo within border states of Mexico. The U.S. will allow Mexican motor carriers the same operations within the border states of California, Arizona, New Mexico, and Texas. During the three-year period, Mexico will allow 49 percent foreign ownership in trucking companies providing international service. After six years of the signing of NAFTA, starting January 1, 2000, the United States and Mexico are to allow complete cross-border access to both countries' interior territory. However, with the easing of entry regulations, immigration laws will not be revised to allow Mexican truckers to conduct point-to-point transport of domestic cargo in the U.S. (cabotage).[14] Mexican investors will be allowed to maintain minority ownership of U.S. companies. Seven years after the signing of NAFTA, Mexicans may have 100 percent ownership in U.S. transporting firms. Ten years after the signing of NAFTA, the Mexican government is to allow 100 percent foreign investment in trucking companies in Mexico (Senate 1993, 7-8; Schulz 1993, 28).

On October 6, 1994, in an apparent move to continue the momentum toward freer trade and less regulatory control over truck movements, President Clinton modified the moratorium placed on inbound Mexican trucks by the Bus Regulatory Reform Act to allow Mexican small package delivery services to operate in the United States so long as Mexican authorities abide by NAFTA (President 1994). Also in 1994, the Trucking Industry Regulatory Reform Act was enacted which removed the states' power to regulate intrastate trucking by eliminating tariff filing requirements (Grimm and Windle 1997, 23). On December 31, 1995, the ICC Termination Act was signed into law which established the Surface Transportation Board (STB); eliminated the distinction between contract and common carriers, and codified the remaining regulation reductions on motor carrier operations. The STB is based in, but independent of, the Department of Transportation; it completely replaces the now defunct ICC (Spychalski 1997; DRI/McGraw-Hill et al. 1998, 22). In an apparent about-face from these actions, on December 18, 1995, the day NAFTA would have opened the U.S.-Mexican border, Transportation Secretary Federico Pena and U.S. Trade Representative Mickey Kantor announced that the opening of the U.S. side of the border will be delayed until Mexican truckers can meet U.S. safety standards (Greenberger 1995, A2). Essentially, this policy action will keep the Motor Carrier Safety Act enacted indefinitely, restricting transborder trucking across the U.S.-Mexican border. Currently, hundreds of requests for U.S. operating authority have been made by Mexican truckers to the Department of

Transportation, but the DOT will not act on them until further negotiations over safety issue are conducted (Barnes 1997, 14).

The truck entry deregulation component of NAFTA, if and when it is enacted, will be the most dramatic change in public policy concerning truck transportation since the Motor Carrier Act of 1980. NAFTA will essentially create competition in a segment of the motor carrier industry where before there was none. The increased competition from Mexican truckers will undoubtedly cause a significant change in the structure of the trucking industry. Inefficient firms will exit the market and remaining firms, as well as new entrants, will be forced to use resources more efficiently.

NOTES

1.   The following paragraph (Childs 1985, 121) elucidates the political mentality of the day concerning regulating utilities and is a telling characterization of Joseph Eastman: "In characteristically independent fashion, . . . Eastman reversed the assumptions implicit in government-business relations in the Progressive Era. Most leading progressives believed the government had the right to control private utilities because their operations affected the general welfare; Eastman, in contrast, saw the utilities as performing tasks the state could (should) have performed. The distinction illuminates Eastman's independent nature and a curious irony. One of the most respected public regulators in American history would have preferred a socialist political economy."

2.   The Motor Carrier Act also regulated interstate transport of persons. This aspect of the Act will not be discussed in this book.

3.   In a humorous example of the almost automatic protest of new applicants, several existing carriers protested the application of a frustrated trucker who filed for permission to haul yak fat. Thirty established motor carriers protested the issuance of the certificate on the grounds that the entering carrier directly affected their existing service. The humor lies in the fact that yak fat cargo was a fictitious commodity (Chapman 1977, 36).

4.   Sloss (1970, 355) estimates from 1958 to 1963, regulated truckers collected more revenue than unregulated truckers at a difference totaling $361 million, or $1.95 billion in 1997 dollars. However, Plamer (1973) successfully criticized these estimates as being over estimations.

5.   Also, see Snow and Sobotka 1977.

6. For an excellent report on the policy changes leading up to 1980 to include the initial effect of MCA, see Interstate Commerce Commission 1981; also Robyn 1987.

7. The Motor Carrier Act of 1980 allowed collective rate making, but the direction of rate making has become increasingly independent. Several of the largest motor carriers withdrew from the rate bureaus to publish their rates. It is apparent that with easier entry into the interstate trucking market collusive price setting is difficult to maintain.

8. The local government around the port of Nuevo Laredo/Laredo has allowed U.S. trucks to transport U.S. cargo within 20 kilometers of the border, but the U.S. trucker must return to the United States empty (House 1987, 42). Molina and Giermanski (1994, 62) note that U.S. truckers with valid commercial drivers' licenses may cross the border for interlining purposes; however, most interlining occurs on the U.S. side of the border.

9. Cabotage (foreign carriers transporting freight between two points within a country) is strictly prohibited in the United States, Canada, and Mexico.

10. In 1982, there were only four Mexican motor carriers who were issued ICC authority to transport goods into and out of the United States; none have 48 state authority (Department of Commerce 1993, 13).

11. In 1976, the Interstate Commerce Commission increased the size of commercial zones, which increased the range where Canadian and Mexican carriers could operate in the U.S. without federal authority. The impetus of expanding the commercial zones was rooted in accommodating domestic commerce. It was not until March 1978, when the Ninth Circuit Court of Appeals in San Francisco heard appeals from a group of short-haul carriers, that the expansion of the commercial zones was allowed (General Accounting Office 1978, 4). The commercial zones were defined in the 1930's on a case-by-case basis. At that time, the areas that constitute the commercial zones were arbitrarily defined by the ICC. The new ruling defined commercial zones based on a mileage-population formula. Depending on the population of the municipalities a band of a given mileage was allowed around the outer limits of the municipalities. The entire municipality and the band made up the commercial zone. If two commercial zones intersect, then the two zones are considered one commercial zone. Truck operations within the commercial zone are exempt from ICC regulations. This new rule allows Mexican motor carriers to transport goods nearly 75 miles into parts of California and Texas.

12.   U.S. Custom Service also imposed a tariff on foreign commercial trucks entering the U.S. as a way to redress the issue of Canada's unfair advantage concerning transborder truck entry prior to 1987 (Gorys 1987, 353).

13.   Approximately 2,300 Canadian motor carriers held ICC operating authority with about 800 of those holding 48-state authority by July 1992. Canadian authority is issued at the provincial level, not the national level. However, in 1991, U.S. motor carriers obtained about 5,300 grants of Canadian provincial authority, compare to 4,300 in 1990. Nearly 2,300 grants of operating authority were issued by Ontario province with only 22 from the Yukon territory.

14.   Anti-cabotage laws have been reduced recently. U.S. Customs ruled that foreign vehicles may make pickups within the U.S. so long as the movement is incidental to the trucks leaving the U.S. (Binkley 1997, 41; Binkley 1998, 38).

CHAPTER 3

Structure of the Trucking Industry

Trucking is by far the dominant mode for the transportation of goods within the U.S. The movement of goods by highway accounts for more revenue than from air, rail, water, and pipeline combined (Dempsey 1991, 255), which is nine times the size of the railroad industry alone (Standard & Poor's 1991, R45). In general, freight transportation makes up approximately 6.3 percent of the U.S. GNP which represents about $400 billion in revenue annually (Teske, Best, and Mintrom 1995, 2). In 1990, the trucking industry accounted for 78 percent of the total freight industry's earned revenue and 41 percent of the total freight industry tonnage (Interstate Commerce Commission 1992, 71). In 1992, the trucking industry generated $281 billion (Department of Commerce 1993, 9).

The motor carrier industry consists of many heterogeneous carriers of various types of cargo with separate legal and service characteristics (Allen and Liberadzki 1987, 11). Prior to the Motor Carrier Act of 1980, regulating truckers in the motor carrier industry was a daunting task. The problems in regulating this industry stem from the difficulty of distinguishing the many forms of trucking. A system was devised to regulate truckers by partitioning the industry into various categories. The system forced truckers to fit into the prescribed categories and limited the truckers' operations outside their partition. Even with forced partitioning of the industry, the continued growth and evolution of the U.S. economy, coupled with the desire of trucking firm owners and managers to adapt to the evolving markets, blurred the lines of distinction in the industry. Over the years, with the growth of the U.S. economy along with the sluggishness of regulatory changes, the constraints on the industry increased the inefficiency of transporting freight, with the average family in 1986 spending approximately $800 ($1,162 in 1997 dollars) for interstate truck transportation alone (Robyn 1987, 15). The public's recognition and policymakers' intolerance of the inefficiency of the transportation system led to the eventual liberalization of interstate motor carrier regulations. This chapter will attempt to distinguish the most common forms of interstate trucking and provide information on transborder trucking. As a starting point, the classification scheme of the industry will follow the basic structure recognized by the Interstate Commerce Commission, but the reader should be aware that the trucking industry is adapting quickly to the evolving needs of the economy and the lines of demarcation in the industry are somewhat nebulous. So, the following discussion will be only a broad overview of the structure of the industry.

Prior to the Motor Carrier Act of 1980, the type of regulations placed on the trucking industry depended on the type of trucking performed. Truckers were issued certificates or permits based on the type of cargo carried and the routes that they took. When the Interstate Commerce Commission screened applications for certification, greater importance was placed on either the routes the trucker traveled or on the cargo that the trucker wished to carry (Snow 1977, 5). Regulating such a diverse industry necessitated the recognition and categorization of the different types of truck transportation in the broadest general terms. Davis (1981, 4-14) developed a workable methodology for classifying the trucking industry in the United States based on the legal identity recognized by the ICC. Davis divided truckers into four categories: common, contract, exempt, and private carriers. Within each of the categories, subcategories further divided the truck classifications based on whether the truckers operated over a regular route or an irregular route.

First are common or general carriers which carry general freight over regular or irregular routes. This category can be segmented into two further categories, less-than-truckload (LTL) and truckload (TL) carriers.

The LTL carriers' shipments are generally smaller than the capacity of a full forty-eight or fifty-three foot trailer (technically their load size is less than 10,000 lbs.). They traditionally require an extensive hub-and-spoke network of routes and terminals to transport and consolidate cargos into loads large enough to efficiently utilize trailer capacity. The average shipment size of an LTL is about 900 lbs.

(Interstate Commerce Commission 1992, 20). The terminals act as consolidation points or freight breakdown points. Local terminals are used to consolidate cargo shipped from nearby businesses. Trucks from the local terminals retrieve the cargo from the businesses and transport it back to the terminals where the cargo is consolidated into truckload lots and transported to a central hub strategically located in the U.S. At the central hub, the cargo is broken down and sorted again into truckload lots to be taken to a local hub near the final destination of the cargo. Once transported to the local terminals the cargo is broken down into smaller shipments and delivered to the final destination. This system is unique in all of ground transport industries and cannot be effectively replicated by any other mode of transportation.[1] In efforts to speed delivery, the hub-and-spoke method is giving way to direct loading where cargo at one hub is delivered directly to the destination hub, bypassing the central hub completely (Standard & Poor's 1997, 11). Prior to deregulation in 1980, these carriers held general commodity certificates of operation. In 1979, of the 17,000 motor carriers regulated, only 1,000 were general commodity carriers. These carriers accounted for nearly two thirds of the revenue of the entire trucking industry (Robyn 1987, 17). Examples of the largest trucking companies in this industry are Yellow Freight, Consolidated Freightway, and Roadway Express, each generating over $2 billion in revenues yearly (Schulz 1998[b], 15). The small package service sector, which specializes in two or three day delivery, is considered separate from the LTL industry. The United Parcel Service (UPS) is the largest player in this industry with revenue of over $10 billion dollars annually (Interstate Commerce Commission 1992, 69).

Research has shown evidence of economies of scale in the LTL branch of the trucking industry. The four-firm concentration ratio increased after deregulation from 23 percent in 1977 to 42 percent in 1987 and concentration appears to be increasing (Kling, 1990). Also, in other countries such as the United Kingdom, where trucking is virtually unregulated, the industry displays increasing economies of scale (Bayliss, 1986).

The truckload (TL) industry consists of carriers with cargo weighing greater than 10,000 pounds. TL's typically haul directly from shippers to receivers without going through sorting terminals. This sector of the trucking industry is highly fragmented; typical cargo composition varies from raw materials to finished goods, and the truckers are normally long distance haulers. The TL industry does not compellingly exhibit economies of scale as it can accommodate new entrances, unlike the LTL industry[2] (see Rakowski 1989; McMullen and Tanaka 1995; Adrangi, Chow, and Raffiee, 1995). Railroads can provide the same service that the TL industry offers; thus, railroads are direct competitors for the TL long distance hauls. The direct competition from railroads contributes to TL rates normally being lower than LTL rates. Often railroads and TL shippers work hand-in-hand in transporting goods by piggybacking trailers on flat cars. Truck trailers are loaded on railroad flat cars and transported near the cargo's final destination. Then the trailer of cargo is transported by truck to its final destination. The TL segment of the trucking industry is the largest both in terms of total tonnage and revenues. The largest TL's are Schneider National, J.B. Hunt, and Landstar. Schneider National has 12 thousand tractors and 35 thousand trailers and is the largest TL carrier with $2.5 billion in annual revenue, J.B. Hunt has a projected $1.7 billion annual revenue, and Landstar has approximately $1.4 billion annual revenue (Schulz 1998[a], 15).

The second category of trucking is contract carriers, which are defined as for-hire truckers producing specialized services to a limited number of shippers. Contract carriers could not transport general public freight during the period of ICC regulation. Brought about by common carriers' insistence that contractors could undercut the regulated rates of common carriers, the ICC placed a floor on the rates that contract carriers could charge (Moore 1972, 30; Robyn 1987, 18). The number of shippers that a trucking company must provide service to before being considered a contract carrier is somewhat unclear. The ICC arbitrarily chose the maximum number of shippers to be eight (Felton and Anderson 1989, 20). The ICC often classified the borderline cases as specialized-common carriers. Examples of contract carriers are truckers transporting wholesale grocery products, mass merchandising, discount products, and other select manufacturing and distributive industries. Because contract carriers hold contracts with shippers, most movements of freight involve one-way hauls, which often caused empty backhauls. As a result of this backhauling problem, the contract carriers require extensive use of freight brokers' services to acquire cargo to fill their trailers on the return trips (Davis 1981, 11).

The third category is exempt carriers. Exempt carriers are truckers who traditionally were free of ICC regulations. Their operations did not require operating authority. They primarily hauled agricultural goods. Their exempt status was a testimony of the political strength of the agricultural community in the 1930's when the trucking industry fell under ICC's regulatory control (Felton and Anderson 1989, 25). Though exempt from most regulations, exempt truckers were often plagued by empty backhauls. They were prohibited from hauling manufactured goods, unless they applied as a common carrier for authorization from the ICC. For an example of the difficulty of acquiring a backhaul, an exempt trucker would be allowed to carry unprocessed agricultural goods to a processing plant but the trucker would be prohibited from transporting the processed agricultural goods on the backhauls. As a consequence of the trucker's exempt status several miles of empty backhauls would occur. After deregulation in 1980, the distinction between exempt trucking and other forms of trucking has faded.

The last category is private carriage. A private carriage is an individual or person who transports his own goods as part of his primary business activity. The regulation of common carriers drove trucking rate above competitive levels; many manufacturers chose to develop their own private trucking fleets (Federal Trade Commission 1988, 5). In 1977, private carriage constituted the largest segment of the trucking industry if measured in ton-miles (Davis 1981, 11). Together the private and exempt carriers constituted 60 percent of the trucking industry in 1978 (Robyn 1987, 19). Today, despite deregulation, private trucking is still the largest segment of trucking accounting for over 44 percent of the trucking industry (Standard & Poor's 1997, 7). Prior to deregulation, these truckers also suffered from empty backhauls. The ICC, in issuing operating authority, placed more importance on the type of cargo that these truckers carried and less emphasis on the routes that they traveled; as a result, empty backhauls were common. Often certification was issued to truckers restricting them to transporting cargo only related to their own business; thus, the private truckers would have to forego backhaul loads that were not a part of the primary business. Today these requirements are substantially weakened, with private carriers enjoying greater freedom in transporting cargo so that empty backhauls are no longer a problem. Their operations have become nearly indistinguishable from common carriers.

Another category of trucking, that is often cited in the literature which is actually a subcategory of common carriers, is specialized carriers. Specialized carriers are generally small firms that specialize in the transportation of truckload shipments. They are in many cases owner-operators. Owner-operators were used extensively by both the TL and LTL firms prior to 1980. Most of the owner-operators operated without ICC certificates. They usually would operate under a lease agreement which allowed them to operate under the leasors' authority (McMullen 1987, 310). Because specialized carriers' equipment is often built to carry specific cargos, prior to 1980 the ICC issued operating authority based on the importance of the commodities that they carried and allowed flexibility in the routes over which they operated. Empty backhauls pledge this industry; as a result, specialized carriers have low trailer utilization levels that have not significantly changed since deregulation in 1980, which makes them unique in the trucking industry (Pustay 1989, 242-3). There is strong evidence that specialized carriers operate in a constant cost industry (Thomas, and Callan 1992; Grimm, Corsi, and Jarrell 1989; Christensen and Huston 1987). Examples of specialized trucking are refrigerated trucks, tank trucks and automobile carriers.

In today's world of liberal issuance of operating authority, shippers of specialized commodities will either provide specialized transport privately or contract out the services. Shippers of specialized cargo over regular routes that have high probabilities of full backhaul loads will most often choose to perform the transportation privately. This would make the trucking service an integrated part of the production process of the firm, indistinguishable from the internal manufacturing operations of the organization (Boyer 1993, 483). With shipping patterns less regular and higher probabilities of empty backhauls, the shippers will often contract out the service. By contracting out the transportation of their freight, the shippers avoid the startup cost associated with providing the service privately. In contracting out the service, the shipper would only be required to pay for the service and depreciation of the equipment used in the supply of transportation for the time of use.

Regardless of whether the cargo requires specialized transport, firms who privately supply their own truck transport may find it economical to contract out services to a for-hire trucker because of higher probabilities of empty backhauls inherent in private trucking. For-hire truckers generally are more adept in utilizing trailer capacity by being able to acquire cargo for backhauls with relative ease. Thus, for-hire truckers are more likely to be able to reduce fronthaul transportation rates by recouping the cost of backhaul movements from another shipper wishing to transport cargo in the other direction. This makes privately supplied transportation, because of the higher probability of empty backhauls, more likely to face higher rates. Traditionally the private trucking sector of the industry is 50 percent larger, as measured in ton-miles, than the for-hire service (and would be even larger if local-pickups and deliveries are included) (Boyer 1993, 483).

The probability of obtaining backhauls domestically within the U.S. has changed substantially after deregulation. This is evidenced by the tremendous increase in the number of transportation brokers entering the market (Crum, 1985). The transportation property brokers are third-party associates who consolidate freight into truckload lots and arrange for the pick-up and delivery of cargo, but they do not normally perform the actual transportation of the shipments. Brokers must hold a security bond. Their liability for loss or damage of cargo is limited to only negligence in arranging for the transportation, and any physical damage to the cargo is usually paid by the shipper (Brown 1984, 9). Unlike shipping associates who just consolidate freight into truckload lots, brokers are usually hired by truckers for their information and expertise in arranging for pickups and deliveries. When truckers face demand uncertainty, trucking firms would have to increase capacity or rely heavily on private motor carriers to satisfy unusually high demand. For unusually low demands, excess capacity results. By using brokers' services, truckers can more efficiently utilize capacity and thus lower their cost (Brown 1995).

Prior to 1980, the regulations placed on the trucking industry forced most truckload motor carriers to internalize the services now provided by brokers. After deregulation trucking firms began specializing solely in the physical transportation of goods, which allowed others to specialize in services to arrange for the transportation of freight. This change in the structure of the trucking industry after deregulation allowed the transportation property broker industry to flourish. In 1980, there were less than 100 licensed brokers. Five years later, in early 1985, there were approximately 4,000 brokers with ICC authority (McMullen and Stanley 1988, 301). In 1986, their numbers exceeded 6,000 (Senate 1987, 1). By July 1991, there were more than 7,100 actively licensed brokers (Interstate Commerce Commission

1992, 73). The increased number of transportation property brokers gives more truckers the ability to buy the services necessary to reduce empty backhauls that were once only afforded to those who could internalize the service or overinvest in capacity.

Related to the freight brokers are freight forwarders. Freight forwarders are third party intermediaries who consolidate LTL freight to take advantage of trailer capacity, but unlike both brokers and shipping associates, freight forwarders take responsibility for the delivery of the cargo (Madras 1989, 135). Freight forwarders are not responsible for posting security bonds as brokers, but they must insure the cargo for loss of damage for the entire movement (Muller 1992, 38-41). Traditionally, the ICC viewed freight forwarders as common carriers, and as such they were heavily regulated (House 1986, 4). Regulation of freight forwarders began in 1942 (Felton and Anderson 1989, 24). It was not until 1986 that freight forwarders were deregulated with the signing of the Surface Freight Forward Deregulation Act.

Freight forwarders and transportation property brokers have effectively competed away some of the market shares of the LTLs by consolidating 5,000 to 10,000 pound loads into full truckloads which are then delivered by TLs (Interstate Commerce Commission 1992, 20). Thus freight forwarders and transportation property brokers bridge the gap between LT and LTL, and create competition between the modes. This competition will undoubtedly have the effect of suppressing the rates that LTL can charge.

The trucking industry broadly defined as for-hire trucking (which includes common, contract, and exempt carriers) exhibits significant economies of scale[3] (Ying 1990[a]; Keeler 1989; McMullen and Stanley 1988; Gagné 1990; McMullen and Hiroshi 1995). The extensive network of the LTL segment of the industry with the high fixed cost of network terminals gives partial explanation of the emergence of economies of scale after deregulation, but other factors must be considered to explain the nationwide increase in concentration of the industry. Most of the entry into the trucking industry has occurred by owner-operated common carriers. Though able to survive at a relatively small scale, the typical case is for new entrants to contract out their services to the larger corporations (Boyer 1993, 484). The advancement of sophisticated satellite tracking of trucks gives large scale trucking companies lower average cost of transporting cargo. This may provide the answer to the increasing concentration but further research in this area is needed.

The trucking industry is also subject to an inverse relationship between price and quality of service. In the U.S., truckers are limited to a total of 80,000 pounds per haul. The pooling of shipments leads to an reverse price/quality tradeoff. The tradeoff exists because by charging lower prices, the trucking firm will be forced to increase equipment and capacity to satisfy demand; thus, the frequency of service (an element of quality) will increase (Boyer 1993, 483). The inverse price/quality relationship also exist in the airline industry (Bennett and Boyer 1990).

Also, truckers face a derived demand curve. Because of this truckers cannot merely lower their price and expect a significant increase the volume of freight shipped. Instead, by lowering rates the truckers are more likely to steal demand away from rival truckers (Dempsey 1991, 307). On the other hand, shippers will consolidate less-than-truckloads to truckload shipments when the price of transport increases, which alters the frequency of trips made by the truckers (Boyer 1993, 482-3).

Table 3-1: Operating Ratio of ICC Truckers for the Years 1980 to 1997

Year	Operating Ratio	Year	Operation Ratio	Year	Operation Ratio
1980	96.0	1986	94.2	1992	95.4
1981	97.1	1987	97.5	1993	95.0
1982	99.2	1988	95.6	1994	95.3
1983	96.2	1989	96.6	1995	96.5
1984	96.2	1990	95.7	1997	98.0
1985	96.3	1991	95.7	average	96.26

Sources: Dempsey, Paul Steven, 1991. Running On Empty: Trucking Deregulation And Economic Theory. *Administrative Law Review* 43(253) (spring): 268, and DRI/McGraw-Hill; Standard & Poor's; U.S. Department of Commerce/International Trade Administration. 1998. Chapter 43 in *U.S. Industry & Trade Outlook*: 23.

Though truckers have the ability to increase and decrease prices in the short run in order to steal demand from their competitors or increase the frequency of shipments, in the long run truckers can expect to make at best a normal rate of return. Table 3-1 lists the operating ratios (non-interest and non-tax operating expenses as a percentage of operating revenues) of common carriers registered with the ICC from 1980 to 1997.

Operating ratios in 1980 were 96.0; in 1997 (an exceptional year for truckers) they were 98.0. Over the 17 years of data, the average is 96.26. If the operating ratios were small, then total revenues would exceed operating cost by a large margin. This would suggest that trucking firms were making excessive profits. Typically carriers with operating ratios less than 90.0 are considered to be making excessive profit (Teske, Best, and Mintrom 1995, 110). Though operating ratios are not profit estimates, the above numbers suggest that truckers can expect at best to earn normal rates of return on their investments. Some price flexibility in the short run and only normal rates of return suggest that the trucking industry more closely represents a monopolistically competitive model.

The size of the labor force in the trucking industry is substantial. In 1991, the U.S. trucking industry employed roughly 238,000 full-time employees (Interstate Commerce Commission 1992, 73). The less-than-truckload industry has captured the limelight in the transportation literature and information on this industry is plentiful. The breakdown of the LTL trucking industry in terms of workforce and compensation is as follows:

Table 3-2: Employment Distribution & Average Compensation Among Primarily LTL and Small Package Carriers

Employment Category	Number	Percent	Compensation
Drivers and Helpers..	181,567	39%	$34,000
Cargo Handlers........	125,863	27%	16,000
Managerial..............	67,865	15%	40,000
Clerical....................	53,205	12%	18,000
Vehicle Rep. & Serv.	17,201	4%	26,000
Officers...................	966	0.2%	104,000
Other......................	14,141	3%	28,000
All Categories...........	460,808	100%	$266,000

Source: Interstate Commerce Commission. 1992. *The U.S. Motor Carrier Industry Long After Deregulation: a Report by the Office of Economics Interstate Commerce Commission.* Table 7. (March): 74.

Drivers and helpers constitute the lion's share of number of the employees in the LTL industry with 39 percent of the total number of employees. Cargo handlers are a close second, making up 27 percent of the industry. Though these two categories together make up 66 percent of the total number of employees in the LTL industry, officers which only make up 0.2 percent of the employed workforce in trucking, earn on average twice the compensation of the other two categories combined. This suggests that the complexity of the LTL operations require skilled managers to organize the flow of traffic.

Deregulation has caused considerable restructuring in the use of labor in the trucking industry. In 1973, of labor employed in for-hire trucking, 60.3 were unionized, and 40.0 percent of labor in private trucking were unionized. In 1995, only 24.9 percent of labor in for-hire trucking and 17.2 percent in private trucking were unionized (Hirsch and Macpherson 1997, 77). Labor is not the only factor of production affected by deregulation. Before the Motor Carrier Act of 1980, regulated firms overutilized capital which is one reason leading to the high wages that existed prior to deregulation (Averch and Johnson 1962; Adrangi, Chow, and Raffiee 1995; Kim 1984; Thomas and Callan 1992). After deregulation, firms started to use capital and labor optimally, which has caused cost to fall by 16 percent per year with continuous productivity gains (Ying 1990[b]) accompanied by rate decreases (Ying and Keeler 1991).

3.1 INTERNATIONAL TRUCKING

Literature on international trucking is woefully lacking, and literature on transborder trucking (transporting good across international boundaries) is nearly nonexistent. With the limitation on information, we know that the structure of Canadian and Mexican domestic trucking is similar to the basic structure of the U.S. domestic industry. U.S. transborder trucking has received little consideration in the economics literature. Though this topic is popular in trade journals, it is only the U.S.-Canadian border that has received attention in academic journals. Canadian transportation specialists have shown interest in transborder trade (Garland Chow being one of the leaders in the field), but few economists have investigated the nature of transborder trucking. Even more neglected in the literature is transborder trucking across the U.S.-Mexican border. This could be due to the fact that very little empirical data exist concerning the movement of goods across the U.S.-Mexican border.

3.1.1 U.S.-Mexico Transborder Trucking

The southern border of the United States is heavily regulated. Trucks from the U.S. are prohibited from crossing the border, and Mexican trucks may cross but their movements are severely limited. The only place in which the two nations' trucks can effectively operate together are within the unregulated commercial zones that surround the ports of entry on the U.S. side of the border. The sole purpose of the commercial zone is for the exchange of freight. The U.S.-Canadian border is nearly unregulated (truckers need only satisfy standard safety and anti-smuggling regulations to cross). Despite these barriers to entry, according to the U.S. Department of Transportation in 1992 approximately 86.6 percent of the total transborder freight between the U.S. and Mexico was transported by means of highway (Department of Transportation 1994, 16). Delays at the U.S.-Mexican border are common. The delays at the port of Laredo, TX, for example, take anywhere from 8 hours to 12 hours to get truck cargo across to Mexico (Matthews 1998, A1; Carroll 1995, A19; Molina and Giermanski 1994, 48). Because Mexico prohibits U.S. trucks into Mexico, one-fifth of all cross-border movements are empty (James 1994, 21). U.S. trucking companies and manufacturers have either established or use the services of third party agents located along the international border who specialize in reducing the cost associated with transborder regulations. According to the Celadon Group, the largest truckload carrier in the U.S./Mexican transborder industry, it is absolutely essential to use a licensed and bonded international broker to get trucks successfully through the maze of regulations at the border (Russell 1998, 16). J.B. Hunt, one of the largest truckload carriers in the U.S., established Hunt de Mexico in El Paso, TX, to help smooth the transference of freight (Gooley 1991, 48). Viking Freight and Roadway Services entered into partnerships with Porter International, a San Diego based broker, to expedite Custom clearing procedures (Schulz 1993, 28). Fawcett and Vellenga (1992, 10) surveyed managers of Maquiladora plants (U.S. assembly plants located in Mexico which export nearly all of their products back to the United States); nearly 75 percent of the respondents used brokers when transporting goods to avoid long delays at the border. In a similar survey by Maltz, Riley, and Boberg (1993), 80 to 90 percent of Maquiladora managers in the El Paso-Juarez area use third party agents in transborder movements. Trade relations over transborder access between the U.S. and Mexico has become much more congenial over recent years, with the signing of NAFTA in 1993, and until recently, transborder movements showed signs of improving.

Historically, the relationship between the U.S. and Canada concerning transborder movements has traditionally been better than U.S./Mexico relations. As a result, transborder truckers have been able to develop cost efficient networks for transporting goods between the U.S. and Canada, but this is not the case for U.S.-Mexican transborder trucking. Though the Mexican transportation sector was deregulated in 1989 (Landero 1990, 106), the Mexican trucking industry is still in the developmental stages. Because of the regulatory constraints on the trucking industry in Mexico and high interest rates on the use capital, the extensive hub-and-spoke network necessary for the existence of low-cost LTL trucking has not developed (Valdes and Crum 1994, 5). Most of the movements of goods in Mexico are point-to-point pickups and deliveries. Mexican truckers do not rely as much as U.S. truckers on third-party associates to organize cargo consolidation. Logistics and warehousing are limited (Farver 1993), though with the improvements in trade relations, U.S. companies are lending their knowledge and expertise to develop efficient logistic systems (Gooley 1991, 48). This is evidenced by research showing that the fastest growing industry in Mexico's economy is the hotels and transportation sector (Mallick and Carayannis 1994). The lack of centrally located transportation brokers in Mexico prevents development of the terminal networks commonly used in the U.S. and Canada. This is similar to the U.S. when regulations forced truckers to internalize the brokerage services. Once deregulated, the hub-and-spoke network quickly expanded in the United States. By Mexican law, imports into Mexico can only be processed by licensed Mexican Customs broker (House 1996, 270; Molina and Giermanski 1994, 53). As a result, most Mexican brokers and freight forwarders locate and focus on intermodal traffic at the border (Burke 1994, 21). Also, drayage companies specializing in the movement of trailers through Customs at border crossings are frequently used in transborder movements (Doyle 1997; Valdes and Crum 1994, 6). These drayage companies are usually small mom-and-pop operations whose trucks are typically older than the trucks used in

Mexico. Normally, their operations involve a full fronthaul and an empty backhaul (House 1996, 275-6).

During the brief period of access to the interior of the U.S. created by the Motor Carrier Act in 1980, Mexican Customs brokers increased their numbers along the U.S. side of the U.S.-Mexican border (Joint U.S.-Mexican. 1982: 63). This implies that resources necessary for the development of networks within Mexico have located along the border. Without the specialization and division of labor in freight consolidation and logistical routing, central Mexican trucking firms will continue to lack the technological advantage of the hub-and-spoke networking that would increase the efficient movement of goods.

Many opponents of NAFTA argue that with the elimination of entry barriers, Mexican carriers will have a cost advantage over U.S. trucking companies, which would force U.S. trucking firms out of the transborder trucking market. Though domestic deregulation has caused unionized wages in the trucking industry to fall (Rose 1987; Hirsch 1988; Peoples 1996; Hirsch and Macpherson 1997), the cost advantage of Mexican labor will not necessarily cause displacement of U.S. trucking firms. NAFTA does not eliminate safety regulations which have in the past restricted most Mexican trucks from entering the U.S. Mexican trucks are typically much older than U.S. trucks. Mexican trucks are reported to be approximately fifteen years old, while U.S. trucks are approximately 5 years old (House 1996, 180). However, reports of the age of Mexican trucks often come from surveys of vehicles entering the U.S. at border crossings (see U.S. General Accounting Office, 1996). Many of these vehicles are older drayage trucks that are used only to transport cargo short distances across the border and are not intended for long distance road travel. There is also a shortage of trailers in Mexico, and it is often cited that service by Mexican truckers is not reliable (Valdes and Crum 1994, 6). Because Mexican law does not require it, most truckers in Mexico do not carry liability insurance (Burke 1994, 21; Russell 1998). Under Mexican law a driver who is involved in an accident can expect to be arrested and jailed for the three days allotted to complete an investigation of the incident (Schiller 1991, 18; Giermanski et al. 1990, 22). Because of Mexico's heavy import controls and high interest rates, the purchase of trucks and spare parts is difficult for most Mexican truckers. A rig that costs $62 thousand in the U.S. costs $80 thousand in Mexico, and banks require truckers to put up front 85 percent of the cost of the vehicle (Senate 1993, 11). Because of central Mexico's underdeveloped trucking network, U.S. trailers are often returned empty to the U.S.-Mexican border, which in essence increases the round trip cost of moving cargo in Mexico (Doyle 1997). The lower labor cost, which is often claimed to be the main cost advantage of Mexican trucking companies, is not as bad as one is led to believe. The average wage for labor involved in the exporting industries in Mexico is approximately 12 percent higher then Mexico's national average (Council of Economic Advisers 1994, 228). Compared to the U.S., Mexican trucking companies do have a 20 percent cost advantage over U.S. firms primarily due to the low cost of Mexican labor. Data from the U.S. Embassy in 1992 indicates that Mexican transborder truckers earn between $35 and $80 a day, which is about 20 percent less than U.S. truckers. The higher wages for transborder trucking in Mexico exist because Mexican truckers who can pass the licensing and safety requirements are highly skilled and thus command a higher wage (General Accounting Office 1993, 2). Mexican labor also receive non-monetary benefits such as meals, transportation to and from work, and groceries (Zurier 1991, 30). Michael Belzer (1995, 654) estimates that U.S. truckload drivers earn between $4.75 to $7.91 per hour, which is in line with Mexican transborder wages. However, using monthly Current Population Survey data, Hirsch and Macpherson (1997, 83) estimate U.S. real hourly wage for the typical union for-hire driver is $15.62; nonunion for-hire driver is $11.71; union private driver is $13.59; and nonunion private driver is $9.70. The recent peso devaluation has benefited the transborder trucking industry in Mexico. Mexican exports have increased faster than their imports, and transborder trucking companies pay labor costs in pesos while revenues are received in high-valued U.S. dollars (Carroll and Torres 1995, A11).

There are differences between Mexico and the U.S. in the legal limit of load sizes. The Mexican legal weight limit on tractor and trailer is 90 thousand pounds while the U.S. weight limit is 80 thousand pounds. The United States' lower weight limits, if enforced, will force Mexican transborder truckers to change their loading practices to ensure compliance with the U.S. laws. Because of insufficient resources in inspecting Mexican inbound trucks, U.S. Custom agents allow many overweight Mexican trucks to enter the U.S., some of which weigh in excess of 150 thousand pounds. The length of trailers allowed in

Mexico may cause problems for U.S. trucking firms. Mexico forbids trailers more than 53 feet in length from operating in Mexico, a length popular in some U.S. states; however, in practice the Mexican law is only minimally enforced (Buckley 1994, 24).

The condition of the interstate road system in Mexico is inferior to the U.S. road system, which contributes to inferior delivery service by Mexican truckers. Many roads are unpaved, and those that are paved are eroded with potholes. The roads have narrow curves that are not satisfactory for trucking and many of the roads have no shoulders (Giermanski et al. 1990, 19). The Mexican government has been working to improve road conditions by funneling funds for their improvement. In a movement toward privatization, entrepreneurs have been permitted to own highways and extract tolls from the users. However, tolls are reported to be extremely high (ranging from 35 to 90 cents per mile), which forces many truckers to use roads of lesser quality to avoid the tolls, which again slows delivery time (Russell 1998).

With primitive road conditions in Mexico, the lack of equipment, and relatively high cost of labor for transborder trucking, it is not at all clear that Mexico has a comparative advantage in the transborder trucking industry.

3.1.2 U.S.-Canadian Transborder Trucking

Prior to 1980, the U.S.-Canadian transborder trucking industry was much more developed than the U.S.-Mexican transborder trucking industry even by today's standards, but it was the Motor Carrier Act of 1980 that increased the Canadian presence in the United States. Canadian trucking networks in the U.S. strengthened. Canadian carriers began their networks at population centers nearest to the U.S.-Canadian border and continued branching deeper into the U.S. after U.S. deregulation. Canadian less-than-truckload (LTL) firms located hubs near the ports of entry and employed U.S. truckers to make U.S.-domestic delivery and pickups (Chow 1995, 11). This gave Canadian transborder truckers an international hub where freight could be consolidated to reduce Canadian carriers' empty haul problems caused by the anti-cabotage laws (Chow 1995, 9-11). Cabotage prohibits Canadian carriers from making pickups and deliveries within the U.S.; thus, reducing Canadians' likelihood of obtaining cargo to haul back to

Canada. Also, because of higher transportation rates in Canada, many Canadian small businesses bypassed the use of Canadian carriers by renting trucks and privately transporting their goods to the border to interline with lower-cost U.S. truckers[4] (Chow 1991, 152). This encouraged U.S. domestic service firms to locate near the ports of entry along the international border, which caused Canadian carriers to lower their rates by as much as 65 percent (Chow 1995, 11).

The Canadian trucking industry is similar to the U.S.; however, there are considerable scale differences. In 1989, the three largest LTL firms in the U.S. had earnings which surpassed the combined earnings of the top thirty-two trucking companies in Canada (Chow 1991, 143). Most of the business activity in Canada is within 200 miles of the border. This geographically restricts the Canadian carriers. Often cited in the literature are claims that the Canadian truckers are handicapped because of their geographically limited area of operation. The claims are that U.S. trucking firms have a comparative advantage over Canadian truckers and could come to monopolize the U.S.-Canadian transborder trucking industry. There is disagreement about the effect that U.S. competition will have on the Canadian trucking industry. Canadians have argued that U.S. transborder truckers dominated the transborder trucking along the northern border. This disagreement came to a head in 1990 and again in 1991 when Canadian owner-operators blocked several main highways into Canada from U.S. carriers. The owner-operators protested against U.S. truckers entering Canada because they felt that the low-cost U.S. carriers were starting to monopolize the industry. However, evidence indicates that Canadian truckers enjoyed a 59 percent share of the transborder market in 1990[5] (Slack 1993, 153). The concerns among Canadian truckers are understandable considering that 18.6 percent of Canadian general freight truckers' revenue is earned through transborder movements; 19 percent of all truckers are solely involved in transborder trucking and generate 54 percent of the total revenue of the Canadian trucking industry[6] (Chow and McRae 1990, 5). In a study by Chow and McRae (1990), they find that Canadian truckers are only disadvantaged in the truckload (TL) industry due their limited geographic location near the international border and the constraints on cabotage in the U.S.

Prior to 1980, interlining international cargo was common with approximately 80 percent of the $1 billion of international bulk freight being interlined at the border (Ellison 1984, 120). Interlining substantially declined after U.S. deregulation. A 1980 investigation of the U.S.-Canadian trucking industry, Ex Parte No. MC-157, showed that in the less-than-truckload sector 13.2 percent of international shipments were single-lined while 86.8 percent were interlined. For the truckload sector, 22.1 percent were single-lined while 77.9 percent were interlined. Ninety-three percent of the truckload freight and seventy-nine percent of the LTL freight transported between the U.S. and Canada originated from the U.S. (House 1983, 145). For Ontario alone in 1980, 47 percent of the revenue from international truck transportation was from jointlined traffic. In 1982, two years after U.S. deregulation, Ontario received only 35 percent of the revenue from international truck traffic (Chow 1995, 11). Comparing this with the interlining performed within the U.S. in 1980, 21.4 percent of all LTL shipments were interlined while 10.2 percent of all TL shipments were interlined (Allen and Liberadzki 1987, 17). This suggests that interlining was a common component of the transborder industry prior to opening the border for truck access. In 1986, over 96 percent of all U.S. truck movements were single-lined (Chow 1995, 11). After the Motor Vehicle Transportation Act (MVTA) of 1987 that deregulated the Canadian side of the border and allowed U.S. trucks to directline shipments into Canada, rate competition increased. Trucking rates on movements outside the provinces, to include transborder movements, were typically higher than intra-provincial movements for the years prior to MVTA. After the MVTA inter-provincial rates fell below intra-provincial rates with the difference increasing over time (Chow 1995, 15). Just as with the U.S. deregulation, after the MVTA, the Canadian trucking industry increased specialization. Truckers relied more on third-party associates (brokers and forwarders) for freight arrangement and consolidation which increased trucking efficiency (Palmer 1988, 72). But even with the unilateral deregulation of the U.S.-Canadian border stemming from the MVTA, the border still seems to matter as trucking rates are substantially higher for transborder movements than for inter-provincial movements (McCallum 1995).

As with Mexico, there are legal constraints on trailer sizes in Canada. Canadian vehicles are allowed a maximum length of forty-one feet. The States of New York and Michigan (states with the busiest ports of entry) restrict vehicles to be a maximum of forty feet (Chow and McRae 1990, 12). The differences in trailer size regulations has not created significant problems for the transborder movement of goods.

3.2 MAJOR ROUTES OF CENTRAL MEXICO

With the exception of the rapidly growing Maquiladora industry along the border, Mexico City is the center of economic activity in Mexico. Industrial and agricultural goods exported from Mexico City to the U.S. travel along well defined trade routes. According to McCray (1993, 6-9), there are four main routes truckers follow from Mexico City to the U.S. as shown in Figure 3-1. Two of the four main routes follow along the eastern and western coast lines of the country while the other two routes are centrally located. The coastal routes are labeled Gulf Coast Route and Pacific Route in Figure 3-1. The Gulf Coast Route starts at Mexico City and runs through Pachuca, Tuxpan, Tampico and up to the port of Brownsville. The proximity of Brownsville near the Gulf of Mexico makes it well suited as a port for water vessels. As a result of this, a large portion of the imports passing through the Brownsville port of entry is carried by water vessels.

The Pacific Route follows from Mexico City to Guadalajara, Tepic, Mazatlan, Los Mochis, Cd. Obregon, Guaymas, and up to the port of Nogales. An offshoot of this route runs along the U.S.-Mexican border to the San Diego ports of entry. The port of Nogales handles predominately agricultural imports. San Diego handles a combination of Maquiladora and agriculture imports originating from the Maquiladora plants near the border and the industries located on the Baja of California peninsula.

The Pacific/Central Route emanates from Mexico City and continues up through Aguascalientes, Zacatecas, Torreon, Chihuahua, and to the El Paso port of entry. The majority of the international trade traveling along this route involves movements of goods between Chihuahua and El Paso where a large concentration of Maquiladora plants are located.

The Central Route is the primary path to transport international trade between central Mexico and the U.S. This route starts at Mexico City travels up through San Luis Potosi, Saltillo, Monterrey, and to the port of Laredo. Over one-half of the trade between the U.S. and Mexico travels along this route (McCray 1993, 8).

The Mexican landscape dictates the path that the routes follow. Mexico can be described as a county with high, rugged mountains, low coastal plains, high plateaus, and desert (Central Intelligence Agency, 1997). Along the west coast of the country, traveling north and south, are the mountain ranges east and west Sierra Madre Occidental. Sierra Madre Occidental west has an elevation that exceeds 3,300 miles and divides the Pacific/Central Route from the Pacific Route. Along the eastern coast, the Serra Madre Occidental east has an elevation that exceeds 4,000 miles and divides the Central Route from the Gulf Coast Route. The Sea of Corte and the Sierra Madre Mountains make transportation from the West Coast to Mexico's heartland difficult. Between the two huge mountain ranges lies the Mexican Plateau, an elevated flatland pock marked with smaller mountain ranges, separating the two central routes. These four routes follow a path of least resistance by channeling the natural canal created by the Sierra Madre Occidental mountain ranges through northern Mexico.

3.3 THE PROCEDURES FOR CROSSING THE BORDER

The procedure for crossing the border for truckers is obviously different depending on which border is crossed. The U.S.-Canadian border is relatively easy to cross. The trucker's freight forwarder must prepare the appropriate documents for the crossing. A standard bill of lading is needed, which clearly identifies the Canadian broker that will handle the Custom clearing procedures. Then the trucker should have a commercial invoice that has the names of the shipper and consignee, a detailed description of the products and their value, and the royalties or material contribution made by the purchaser. Though not completely necessary, the commercial invoice should be in both French and English. Next a truck must ensure that the import broker receives a certification of origin. This document is necessary for assessing the duties to be placed on the imported goods. It is recommended that truckers carry all documents with them when crossing the border. At the border, the trucker with the bill of lading and a Canada Custom Invoice in hand will advance to the Customs broker next to the check point. The broker assigns the appropriate import duties, service tax, and service charges to the invoice. Then the trucker awaits for the Custom agents to inspect the documents for clearance. Once cleared the trucker can proceed into Canada (Gooley 1993, 90A-91A). This procedure lasts only a few minutes with few problems. Even with mistakes on the documents that may cause the shipment not to proceed through Customs, shippers can easily fax corrected documents to the Customs broker and mistakes are corrected within minutes. Recommendations are underway to streamline the border crossing requirements even further by having the Custom official conduct checks before the trucks reach the border (Tabburri 1995, A14).

In contrast, the method of advancing cargo through Mexican Customs is not easy. The documentation needed to ensure that shipments will make it through Mexican Customs include: a bill of lading that has the names and phone numbers of the U.S. freight forwarder and Mexican Customs brokers clearly listed on the document, and a commercial invoice that must be in English and Spanish. This document must include a clear description of the goods being imported—abbreviations, product names or codes do not suffice. Also, the full names, and addresses of the Mexican Customs brokers handling the shipment must be on the invoice. Most importantly the Mexican tax identification number must be on the invoice. Without the tax number the shipment is not allowed through Customs. Most of the documents are sent by the forwarder or broker electronically and electronic confirmation is obtained prior to the truck reaching the border. Normally eight copies of the documents will be carried by the trucker. A shipper's export declaration, which must be in Spanish, is necessary, along with other documentation insuring that the product meets Mexico quality standards. All duties must be pre-paid before the cargo can cross the border (Lasky 1995).

The procedure for a trucker's cargo to move through Mexican Customs involves several people, and Custom agents are particular about the exact wording on the import documents. Freight forwarders should receive the documentation by fax prior to the truck leaving the factory so the forwarders can start the process before the trucker reaches Customs. The freight forwarders check the documents for accuracy and hand the documents to the Mexican Custom brokers. The broker adds duties, Customs user fees, value added tax, and the broker's handling fee. Copies of the charges and duties are handed to the U.S. freight forwarder and the consignee. Only when the broker receives the full payment of the duties and handling fee is the cargo permitted to pass through Customs. The broker then pays the Custom agency the appropriate duties and transfers the documentation. Once at the border crossing with the original documents in hand, the trucker hands over the shipment and the export declarations to a local cartage agent (draying company) which takes the cargo through Customs, as U.S. trucks are prohibited in Mexico. The drayer hands the

Figure 3-1: Major Routes from Mexico City to the United States

Source: McCray, John C. 1993. *Trucking Transportation Opportunities and the North American Free Trade Agreement*. Fig. 6. Presented to the 1993 American Trucking Association Management Conference. 1 Nov.: 6. and *Road Atlas.* Rand McNally.

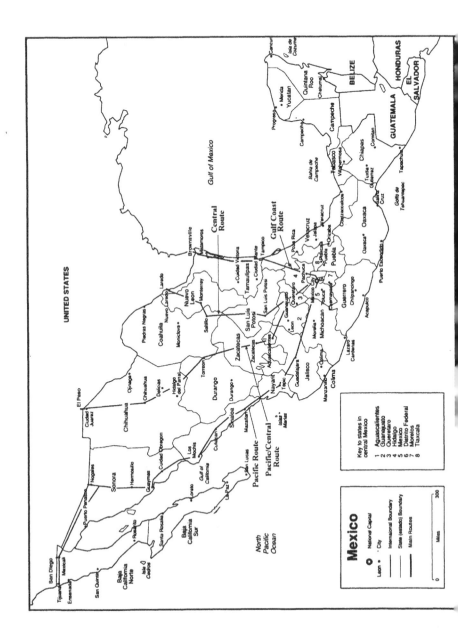

documentation to the Mexican broker, and if the documents match the approved faxed documents, the shipment goes to a red and green stoplight and the trucker pushes a button. If the stoplight shows a green light the trucker may transfer the shipment to a Mexican trucker who will deliver the shipment to its final destination. If the light turns red the trucker must pull over into an inspection yard for a 100 percent search of the cargo (Gooley 1993, 92A) Approximately 90 percent of the trailers are inspected. There is an additional 26-kilometer checkpoint where documents, driver's license, and safety inspection are again undertaken (Russell 1998). These procedures are very time consuming. The inspection process was often the point in which Customs officials would elicit bribes from the shippers (Gooley 1993, 94A). With the recent crackdown on Customs agents accepting illegal bribes, the Mexican government has taken steps to prevent this from happening. The process of shipping goods into Mexico is so long that often hundreds of trucks wait in line for hours just to reach the border (Gooley 1991, 47). At the Laredo, TX, border crossing, trucks often wait anywhere from eight to twelve hours (Carroll 1995, A19). With the signing of NAFTA, Customs officials on both sides of the border are moving toward speeding up the Custom clearing process by having trucks checked prior to reaching the port of entry. However, due to safety concerns, the transborder trucking component of NAFTA has been delayed and there are now reports that crossing points have become more congested and burdensome as Customs inspections have intensified.

NOTES

1. The airline industry works in a similar manner in the passenger transport industry.

2. One must be careful making such a statement. Some studies find economies of scale in both TL and LTL industries (Koenker 1977; Keeler 1989). Adrangi, Chow, Raffiee (1995) and Grimm, Corsi, and Jarrell (1989) find no economies of scale in either the TL nor LTL industry. Harmatuck (1991) finds no economies of scale within the LTL industry, but Kling (1988) suggests that LTL industry must have economies of scale to explain the increasing concentration ratios since deregulation.

3. Other sources find economies of scale for only small firms (Harmatuck 1981). Others cite significant cost changes in this industry as a result of

technological shifts after deregulation (Daughety and Nelson 1988) as well as the presence of economies of scale (Emerson, Grimm, and Corsi 1991).

4. Sloss (1970) found from 1958 to 1963 Canadian regulated truckers' rates were significantly higher than non-regulated Canadian truckers which represented a difference of $15 million per year ($81 million per year in 1997 dollars)

5. Apparently Canadian truckers have always dominated the transborder industry. Gorys (1987) reports that from 1972 to 1984, Canadian truckers had over 50 percent of the transborder trucking market.

6. Statistics Canada (1996, 33 & 61) reports that in 1996, transborder movements accounted from 16 percent of all Canadian truck movements, which makes up 36 percent of total revenue. Also, Canadian trucks carrying 58 percent of their exports to and 80 percent of their imports from the U.S.

CHAPTER 4

Transborder Truckload Size

Unlike domestic trucking, transborder truck movements can exceed the boundaries of a country's regulatory authority. Only when transborder truckers enter a country governed by a regulatory authority can their movements be regulated by the authorities. There are basically two forms of regulations that regulatory authorities impose on foreign truckers: entry barriers and laws against cabotage. The entry barriers prevent foreign truckers from entering the country governed by the regulators. The barriers are placed at the ports of entry and cannot be avoided by circuitous routing. Thus, most transborder truckers are forced to interline shipments at the ports of entry. Rules against cabotage prevent foreign truckers from transporting cargo from point to point inside the regulators' country. This means a foreign trucker entering a country prohibiting cabotage can drop off freight, pick up freight, turn around and leave the country. If the transborder trucker cannot find a load to pick up at or near the drop-off point in the foreign country then the trucker may have to travel home empty. Of course, the transborder trucker can travel empty from one point to another point within the foreign country to pick up cargo to take back to their home country, but such movements are costly and would be performed only if it were economically viable.[1] Thus, in the U.S., because foreign truckers cannot engage in cabotage, the probability of having empty backhauls is high. The greater likelihood of having an empty backhaul will change the amount of cargo the truckers carry on fronthauls into the United States. Thus, regulations that restrict foreign truckers from entering the U.S. force the foreign truckers to interline shipments, while the laws against cabotage increase the probability of empty backhauls.

NAFTA will reduce entry barriers into the U.S., but the laws against cabotage will remain intact. Opening the border for transborder movements between the U.S. and Mexico will allow truckers to direct-line cargo between the two countries. The direct-lining of shipments will undoubtedly reduce the cost of each transborder movement which in turn will have an effect on the optimal amount of cargo transborder truckers choose to haul. The purpose of this chapter is to model the behavior of transborder truckers and predict the optimal truckload sizes that the truckers choose to transport into the U.S. under different regulatory regimes. The predictions will be tested by analyzing past transborder regulatory regimes and comparing the model's predictions to the actual load sizes carried by transborder truckers.

This chapter will give a brief history of past transborder trucking regulations, then a description of the basic transborder trucking problem, followed by a theoretical model of the optimal load size that transborder truckers choose to haul under different regulatory conditions. An econometric model will be formulated and a discussion of the estimates of the truckload sizes entering the U.S. under different regulatory regimes will conclude the analysis.

4.1 HISTORY OF TRANSBORDER ENTRY REGULATIONS

Prior to the Motor Carrier Act of 1980, both the U.S.-Mexican border and the U.S.-Canadian border were unilaterally regulated. Foreign truckers had to apply for federal permission to enter the United States. Permission was difficult to obtain. The majority of the foreign transborder truckers' movements were limited to the commercial zones around the ports of entry along the two borders for the sole purpose of interlining shipments. After the Motor Carrier Act of 1980, entry into the U.S. became relatively easy. Foreign truckers were permitted to travel deeper into the U.S., but U.S. transborder truckers were prohibited from traveling into either Mexico or Canada.

The period of relaxed U.S. entry regulations did not last long for Mexican transborder truckers. The Bus Regulatory Reform Act of 1982 and the Motor Carrier Safety Act of 1984 increased the regulations on entry by Mexican truckers into the U.S. This forced Mexican transborder truckers to interline with U.S. truckers at the border.

In 1987, Canada signed the Motor Vehicle Transportation Act which deregulated the Canadian side of the U.S.-Canadian border, making the border unilaterally free of entry barriers. This permitted U.S. carriers to compete on equal ground with the Canadian truckers in the transborder market. U.S. truckers were allowed to transport cargo across the northern border with little regulatory interference, thus reducing the Canadian carriers' competitive advantage.

4.2 THE BASIC TRANSBORDER TRUCKING PROBLEM

To understand the nature of transborder trucking and the regulations placed on the industry, the complexity of the transborder trucking process must be reduced to its basic structure for tractability. The basic production process for transborder trucking involves two movements: a fronthaul and a backhaul. To be considered a transborder movement, the cargo hauled must be destined for a foreign country. To simplify the basic elements of the process, transborder trucking can be modeled as a series of nodes connected by lines. The nodes represent places of destination and the lines connecting the nodes are the roads traveled by the transborder truckers. For example, consider Figure 4-1.

Suppose there are two identical truckers, a trucker N and a trucker S. Trucker N resides in country N which consists the nodes A-B-F, and the interconnecting roads. Trucker S resides in country S which consists of nodes C-B-E, and the interconnecting roads. For simplicity, assume that all roads connecting the nodes are the same length. Let node B represent the port of entry between the two countries. The authorities of country N can only regulate the trucking activities between the nodes A-B-F, and the authorities of country S can only regulate the trucking activities between nodes C-B-E.

Suppose neither countries' authorities choose to regulate trucking activities. Trucker N from node A with cargo destined to node C can direct-line cargo to node C and pass node B without stopping. Once at node C, the trucker must drop off the cargo and return to his/her home country, country N, to complete the production process which consists of a fronthaul and a backhaul.

Rules against cabotage play an important role in the production process. First suppose that there are no rules against cabotage. If trucker N finds that there is no cargo at node C to backhaul to country N, then the return trip home will be without cargo. However, with cabotage being legal, the trucker can transport cargo between nodes C and E until

Figure 4-1: Basic Elements of Transborder Trucking

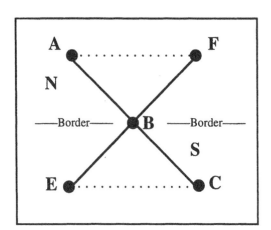

a load is available to haul back to country N. That is, the trucker transports cargo domestically within country S until a load is found to transport back to country N. In this way the trucker would not endure an empty backhaul. The domestic movements are not transborder movements and as such are not technically a part of the fronthaul and backhaul components of the transborder trucking production process.

Now, suppose that both countries forbid cabotage. This restricts trucker N from transporting cargo between node C and node E, and trucker S is restricted from transporting cargo between nodes A and F. The dotted lines between these nodes indicate that only the truckers domiciled in that country can transport goods over these roads. Under the same scenario, once at node C, trucker N cannot deliver cargo to node E, since the rules against cabotage prohibit this activity. Therefore, once at node C, trucker N would have to travel to at least node B empty (or travel empty to node E) to complete the transborder production process. Of course, if there is cargo at node C destined for country N, then the trucker can haul node C's cargo back to country N. We can say, with reasonable assurance, when cabotage is prohibited the likelihood of empty backhauls increases for foreign transborder truckers. Trucker N will incorporate this higher probability of empty backhauls into his/her decision process when choosing the amount of cargo to haul on each round trip. We will find later in this section that a transborder trucker will alter the fronthaul load to compensate for the higher probability of an empty backhaul.

Continuing with the assumption that cabotage is illegal, the spatial dimension of the transborder trucking problem can be reduced. In fact, the above model can be reduced to a system of three nodes connected by a single line. Assume that a trucker can always find a load within its own country to transport internationally by simply transporting domestically until one becomes available. Thus, with probability equal to one, the trucker can secure an international fronthaul. Acquiring an international shipment in a foreign country prohibiting cabotage is less probable. When the trucker is in an anti-cabotage country, the trucker must rely on the chance of having an international shipment at the drop-off point of the fronthaul to transport back to the home country or travel some distance empty. Since a trucker is constrained from engaging in domestic movements of cargo within a foreign country, the probability of securing a backhaul load is less than one. Interpreting the ease of obtaining a backhaul in a foreign country as the truckers assigning the probability distribution over the nodes in the foreign country, the system of nodes and roads can be reduced to a line and represented as follows:

Figure 4-2: Simplified Elements of Transborder Trucking

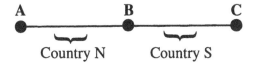

Trucker N transporting cargo from node A to node C would expect a backhaul load at node C with probability of θ (< 1). The a priori expected backhaul load size at node C would be θq, where q is the optimal load size with certainty and θ is the trucker's best guess of the probability of a backhaul at node C. Assuming trucker N and trucker S are identical, trucker S would have the same expectations at node A. Thus, when either trucker transports cargo to a node in the other trucker's country, when cabotage is outlawed, they expect the probability of a backhaul will be less than unity.

Lets now introduce entry barriers into this framework. If the authorities in both countries wish to restrict foreign truckers from entering their country, the authorities would construct barriers to entry in the form of regulations at node B. The entry barriers can be asymmetric or unilateral. If the entry barriers are asymmetric, then one side of the border would be closed allowing only the truckers on the other side of node B to single-line transborder shipments. For example, if the authorities of country N regulate entry, but country S does not, trucker N would be able to transport cargo past node B, but trucker S would be forced to interline at node B. If the entry barriers are unilateral then neither trucker would be able to transport goods past node B, and all international shipments would be interlined. Interlining requires that resources be spent for a successful exchange of loads between truckers. This would increase the cost of transporting international shipments by the amount of resources necessary to interline the shipments. Thus, entry barriers increase the cost to the truckers of transporting cargo across the international border. The change in the cost of transporting cargo internationally will alter the transborder truckers' decisions to haul larger loads. To understand this more clearly, the next section presents the cost structure of a representative transborder trucker in a monopolistically competitive industry. The model will illustrate the effect that entry barriers have on the trucker's decision of how much cargo to carry.

4.3 THEORETICAL ANALYSIS

In general, the trucking industry is characterized by low levels of concentration (Boyer 1993, 484), and individual trucking firms have some flexibility in setting prices in the short-run. Modeling trucking as perfectly competitive does not fit the characteristics of the industry. Service quality varies substantially among carriers, and because shippers are very sensitive to service quality, carriers offering the highest quality gain at the expense of low quality carriers (Allen and Liu 1995). The existence of high and low quality carriers is evidence that consumers perceive differences in the type of service offered by the carriers and are willing to pay different amounts based on the type of service. Given that the carriers' products are both horizontally and vertically differentiated[2] and trucking firms make only normal profits, the trucking industry most closely resembles that of the monopolistically competitive model. By incorporating the monopolistically competitive model with the simplified linear transborder model above, the changes in optimal load sizes transported by transborder truckers can be determined.

In the absence of the cost of interlining, the cost structure of an average transborder trucker in a monopolistically competitive industry is unaffected by whether shipments are interlined or single-lined. However, if there are fixed costs associated with interlining, the average cost of interlining will be greater than the average cost of single-lining transborder shipments,[3] and this will alter the optimal load size truckers carry.

It is the fixed cost of interlining that affects the optimal amount of cargo that truckers choose to haul.[4] Consider a fronthaul from node A in country N to node C in country S where entry barriers are symmetric at node B. Trucker N, faced with entry barriers at node B, would transport cargo from node A to node B and interline the shipment with a trucker in country S, who would transport the cargo to node C. Assume for the moment that interlining is costless. The market forces in a monopolistically competitive industry would cause the price of transborder fronthauls to be high enough to cover the cost of transporting cargo from node A to node B, and also cover the cost of transporting the cargo from node B to node C by another trucker. At this price, economic profits would be zero. Were there no entry barriers at node B, trucker N could transport the cargo directly to node C without interlining, but here again, the market price would have to be high enough to cover the cost of transporting along the segments A-B and B-C such that economic profits are zero. If truckers N and S have identical cost structures, with no fixed cost for interlining, the market price and the optimal fronthaul load size would be unchanged whether shipments are joint-lined or single-lined. Thus, with identical truckers in a monopolistically competitive industry, and in the absence of interlining costs, it makes no difference whether transborder cargo is interlined or not.

However, if there are fixed costs of interlining at node B, then the average cost of joint-lining a fronthaul would be greater than single-lining the cargo. In this case, the market price of transborder trucking would be higher, thus affecting the optimal amount of cargo hauled by the trucker. To see this more clearly consider Figure 4-3.

The average cost to a representative trucker, trucker N, for transporting cargo from node A to node C, with costly interlining at node B, is represented by the curve AC_0. Curve AC_0 is the sum of the average fixed cost associated with transborder trucking (which includes the cost of interlining) plus the average variable costs of transporting cargo between the two terminal nodes.[5] The average load size is denoted by q_0, and the equilibrium market price for transborder trucking would be P_0. A higher price, given the same level of quality, would cause incumbent firms to earn positive economic profits and entry into the market would occur, forcing the market price downward. A price lower than P_0 would cause incumbent firms to suffer economic losses, and exits from the industry would force the market price to increase. Thus, at P_0 incumbent firms make zero economic profits and the market would be in equilibrium with a large number of truckers each transporting q_0 amount of cargo internationally.

If entry barriers are removed from country S's side of node B, then trucker N could transport the fronthaul-cargo directly to node C and avoid the interlining fixed cost. Thus, the average fixed cost of transborder trucking would decrease, causing the average total cost to fall to AC_1 for trucker N. At the original market price P_0 and q_0 amount of cargo, trucker N would be making a positive economic profit and entry into the market would occur. The entry of new firms would reduce the demand for the representative trucker's service to D_1. The equilibrium market price would fall to P_1 and at this price entry into the market would stop. The new entrants would be solely truckers from country N. Truckers in country S would be operating with the higher average cost, AC_0, which makes it impossible for the truckers in country S to compete in price with the lower cost truckers from country N. Thus, the truckers in country S would leave the market—being replaced by new entrants from country N. For simplicity assume entering and exiting the transborder market is free. In the long run, the truckers from country S would completely exit the market to conduct domestic transport only, leaving the transborder movements solely to truckers from country N. At the market price of P_1, the fronthaul load size carried by the representative trucker from country N would fall from q_0 to q_1.

Figure 4-3: Transborder Fronthauls With and Without Interlining Cost

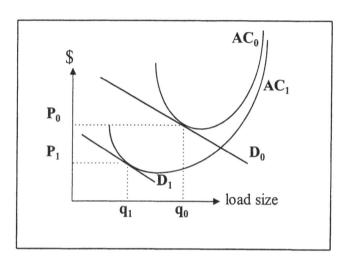

The load size q_1 would be approximately the same for both fronthauls and backhauls for the truckers from country N because the truckers have lower average cost of transporting cargo and can charge a lower price to transport international cargo than the truckers from country S. The profit maximizing shippers in country S would choose the lowest cost trucker to transport their shipments, ceteris paribus. Knowing this, the truckers from country N would revise upward their expectations of the probability of acquiring a backhaul load at node C in country S. For simplicity, assume that the revised probability is equal to one.[6] Under this assumption the fronthaul and backhaul load sizes of the truckers from country N would be the same. Therefore, if entry barriers are reduced on one side of the border, the non-restricted truckers would reduce both fronthaul and backhaul load sizes to approximately the same size.

This situation could be used to model the 1980 Motor Carrier Act. The MCA of 1980 reduced the barriers to entry on the U.S. side of the southern and northern borders of the United States. The Act allowed Mexican and Canadian carriers to avoid interlining fronthauls at the international borders by direct-lining the cargo straight into the U.S.

The theory predicts that MCA would cause Mexican and Canadian truckers to decrease their load sizes on their fronthauls into the United States.

If the regulatory authorities of country S invoke entry barriers at node B then the truckers from country N would be forced to interline again at the border. This would cause the fixed cost of fronthauling to increase for the truckers from country N, and the equilibrium market price would increase again to P_0, and load sizes would increase to q_0.

The Bus Regulatory Reform Act of 1982 and the Motor Carrier Safety Act of 1984 increased the barriers to entry for Mexican truckers entering the U.S.; thus, the model predicts that Mexican truckers would increase their load sizes destined for the United States. This is just the reverse of the situation where the entry barriers were removed.

Now consider the sequential lifting of the barriers to entry at node B which will ultimately lead to the unilateral deregulation of barriers to entry by both countries. Suppose that the barrier to entry at node B is lifted for the truckers from country N. The average cost of transborder trucking would fall and the market price would be P_1 as depicted in Figure 4-3, and the truckers from country N would transport q_1 load sizes on both front- and back-hauls. Now, suppose the authorities of country N deregulate entry for truckers from country S. The deregulation allows the truckers from country S to single-line cargo into country N. The direct-lining reduces the fixed costs of transborder trucking and the average cost of the truckers from country S would decrease. Assuming identical truckers, the average cost curve of the truckers from country S would also fall to AC_1. The truckers from country S will enter the transborder market once again. Even with the same average cost per load, it is not the case that load sizes of the truckers will be q_1. When the border is unilaterally deregulated and both countries' truckers can direct-line cargo to the other trucker's country, the laws against cabotage will become a constraining factor.

Because the cost of transborder trucking is the same for both sets of truckers, and both sets of truckers can direct-line shipments to the others' country, truckers will revise downward their estimates of the probability of obtaining a backhaul once inside the other truckers' country. When country N deregulates entry and the truckers from country S are entering the market, once inside country N, the representative trucker from country S would have to compete with the truckers from country N, who have the same average cost for transporting international cargo. If we assume that shippers are indifferent between the nationality of the truckers, the shippers in country N would be indifferent between the two truckers offering the same service at the same price for transporting international shipments. Because the truckers from country N are domiciled in country N, the anti-cabotage laws would not affect them in their own country. However, since trucker S is prohibited from engaging in cabotage once inside country N, trucker S would be at a disadvantage in obtaining cargo for a backhaul out of country N and would revise his/her expected probability of a backhaul downward. Thus, before transporting a fronthaul load to node A, trucker S would expect a load size of θq_1 as a backhaul, $(\theta < 1)$. Thus, at a market price of P_1, transporting θq_1 amount of cargo from node A to node C would cause the incumbent truckers from country S to take an economic loss on the backhaul. To compensate for the loss, trucker S would increase the size of the load carried on the fronthaul such that the balance of two loads would yield an economic profit of zero (this argument is symmetric with respect to trucker N).

This can be explained in more detail with the use of Figure 4-4. Figure 4-4 represents two graphs in one. The overlaying graphs are of the cost and demand conditions for fronthauls and backhauls of a representative trucker. The superscript F denotes fronthauls, the superscript B denotes backhauls.

Let us generalize the analysis and allow more than one trucker to perform fronthaul and/or backhaul movements. It will be assumed for now that enough time has passed such that entry has occurred, and the market is in equilibrium with an equal number of trucks from both countries conducting the transborder movements.[7] First consider the backhaul problem facing the truckers from country N once inside country S. The truckers know that they cannot engage in cabotage inside a foreign country and will reduce their expectations of getting a backhaul from within country S. Therefore, before transporting cargo to node C, each trucker from country N anticipates a load size of $q^B = \theta q_1$ for a backhaul to transport home once inside country S. At the load size q^B the truckers from country N can expect to take an economic loss of $\Pi(\theta)$ for the haul.

In a symmetric world, the price charged for hauling a load out of country S by the truckers of country N must be the same as the price

Figure 4-4: Transborder Fronthaul and Backhaul with Unilateral Deregulation

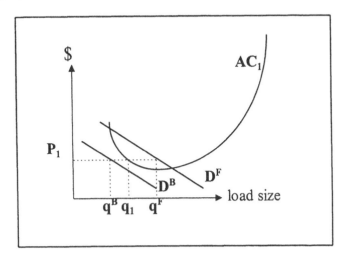

charged by the truckers of country S. The reason is the competition for backhaul loads for the truckers from country N is the same competition that the truckers of country S face for fronthaul loads. The price charged by the country N truckers for backhauling a load out of country S cannot be higher than P_1 in equilibrium. A higher price than P_1 would reduce the demand for their services and increase the demand for the services of the truckers from country S charging the price P_1. The shippers in country S are indifferent between the truckers offering the same service and will choose the trucker with the lowest price to transport their goods. The truckers of country S cannot charge a price higher than P_1 because the truckers from country N can charge a price of P_1 and steal Customers from country S's truckers. Collusion in setting high prices is impossible given the low cost of entering the market by new firms and the large number of truckers already in the market. A price lower than P_1 is not sustainable given that truckers of country S would match prices rather than lose demand. At the lower price, the losses incurred by both sets of truckers would be greater, and in the long-run the threat of bankruptcy would force the truckers to minimize losses. Thus, the equilibrium price for transporting fronthaul and backhaul loads must be P_1. For the representative trucker in Figure

4-4, the equilibrium price and quantity of backhauls is represented by the point (P_1, q^B) on the demand curve D^B.

Because of the expected losses from backhauls, the truckers from country N will choose to carry heavier loads on their fronthauls. The truckers will choose $q^F = (2-\theta)q_1$ amount to carry.[8] The price of the fronthaul shipments must be P_1, and at a price of P_1 the truckers will make just enough profit to compensate for the losses from the backhauls. A price higher would cause truckers from country N to lose fronthaul shipments to the truckers from country S looking for backhauls. A price lower then P_1 would not allow the fronthaul profits to compensate for the expected losses from the backhauls. Thus, each trucker from country N will transport a truckload of size q^F for a fronthaul and earn a profit of Π, and in equilibrium for a monopolistically competitive market the sum of the economic profits and losses from both front- and backhauls would be zero. A positive sum of profits would cause entry into the market; a negative sum of profits would cause exits from the market. Neither case would be an equilibrium condition; so, the sum of the profits must be zero ($\Pi+\Pi(\theta) = 0$). This implies that the expected value of a load for both trips, front- and back-haul, would be $E(q^F + q^B) = 2q_1$. Therefore, with unilateral deregulation of entry barriers, under the assumption that anti-cabotage laws reduce the probability of truckers getting backhauls in a foreign county, it is expected that transborder truckers will carry larger fronthaul loads to compensate for the smaller expected backhaul loads.

Now consider the dynamic adjustments toward equilibrium involved in the sequential lifting of entry barriers. After the eventual lifting of the entry barriers, there would be an equal number of truckers from both nations operating in the transborder market. Prior to the lifting of both barriers, one side of the border was closed to the truckers from country S preventing them from competing with the truckers from country N. Thus, the country N truckers were allowed to transport into country S but truckers from country S could not transport into country N. The number of truckers from country N dominated the market and the truckers from country S resorted to solely domestic trucking. Now, assume barriers into country N are removed for country S's truckers; truckers from country N find backhauling difficult. Once the disadvantage of obtaining cargo for backhauls out of country S from the removal of entry barriers is realized, the truckers from country N would have to increase fronthaul loads to compensate for the expected lighter backhauls. However, if the truckers from country N dominate the market, increasing fronthaul loads is not possible because they ship all the cargo out of country N as it stands. This would imply that truckers from country N would be losing profit on their backhaul loads that are not compensated by increased fronthaul revenues. The combined profit from both front- and backhauls, in this case, would be negative ($\Pi+\Pi(\theta)< 0$). Some of the truckers from country N would exit the industry, allowing the remaining firms to increase their fronthaul loads marginally. Given the limited amount of available cargo in any given country at any given time, the exiting truckers from country N would also allow entry of truckers from country S. The entry and exit process would continue until there are an equal number of truckers[9] from both countries operating in the market such that the extra amount of cargo carried on a fronthaul is exactly the amount of cargo that the other truckers will lack on their backhaul. An equilibrium condition for the sum of the fronthaul (F) and backhaul (B) movements of any two representative truckers from country N and S will have to be ($q_N^F + q_N^B$) = ($q_S^B + q_S^F$) = ($\theta q_N^F + q_S^B$) = ($q_N^B + q_S^F$) = {(1 θ)q_1 + θq_1)} = $2q_1$, where the subscripts denote the country of the truckers and the superscripts represent the type of haul. Depending on how fast trucking firms update their expectations of the probability of backhauls in a foreign country after deregulation and the speed at which entry and exit are physically possible, truckers from country N will continue to dominate the market.

This situation best characterizes the Motor Vehicle Transportation Act of 1987. The Canadian MVTA opened the U.S.-Canadian border for U.S. truck entry while Canadian truckers already had access to the U.S. Depending on how fast U.S. trucking firms enter the transborder market we would expect to find Canadian truckers continuing to dominate the market, with fronthauls entering the U.S. increasing in weight relative to the backhaul loads transported out of the U.S. In equilibrium, Canadian (U.S.) truckers would enter the U.S. (Canada) with heavier loads and leave the U.S. (Canada) with lighter backhaul loads.[10]

To summarize the predictions made above, we should see empirically a reduction in load sizes carried by trucks entering the U.S. across both borders because of the reduction of entry barriers caused by the Motor Carrier Act of 1980. We would expect the reverse to occur after the Bus Regulatory Reform Act of 1982 and the Motor Carrier

Sáfety Act of 1984 closed the U.S. border to Mexican truckers. That is, Mexican inbound truckload sizes should increase because of the restrictive nature of these policies. The Canadian Motor Vehicle Transportation Act which opened the Canadian side of the U.S.-Canadian border to U.S. truckers (making the border unilaterally deregulated) should increase the load sizes of Canadian inbound truckers entering the U.S. while their backhaul would be lighter. This is reverse for U.S. truckers. U.S. truckers should backhaul light loads out of Canada while fronthauling heavier loads into Canada.

4.4 THE DATA

Published historical data on the actual load sizes of foreign truckers entering the U.S. do not exist. Because of the lack of precise data on load sizes carried by trucks entering the U.S. we must construct a proxy. Since nearly 80 percent of the dollar value of imports from both Mexico and Canada entering the U.S. are carried by trucks, dividing the dollar value of imports by the number of trucks entering the U.S. will serve to approximate the average transborder truckload sizes.[11] The annual dollar value of imports crossing the U.S.-Mexican and the U.S.-Canadian borders from the years 1978 to 1993 is measured by Custom value.[12] The Foreign Trade Division of the Bureau of the Census publishes the current Custom value of imports by Custom districts (FT990 and FT920). Data on eight Custom districts will be used to test the predictions made above. Data were collected from four Custom districts along the U.S.-Mexican border and four custom districts along the U.S.-Canadian border. The four districts along the U.S.-Mexican border are San Diego, CA; Nogales, AZ; El Paso, TX; and Laredo, TX. The four districts along the U.S.-Canadian border are Pembina, ND, Detroit, MI, Buffalo, NY, and Ogdensburg, NY. These districts were chosen because they include the largest land ports of entry along the two borders, and they also include more land ports of entry than other districts. The other districts include several inland and sea ports of entry. The eight above districts record mostly imports transported by land vehicles of which trucks are the dominant mode.

For inbound trucks, the U.S. Department of Customs keeps records on the number of inbound trucks passing through each port of entry along the U.S. borders. The number of inbound trucks crossing the four busiest ports of entry (one from each district) along each border will be used to approximate the total number of inbound trucks crossing at all the ports of entry within the four Custom districts.[13]

The proxy for truckload sizes entering the U.S. is the sum of the current Custom value of imports from the Custom districts along each border, deflated by the U.S. GDP deflator, and divided by the sum of the number of inbound trucks crossing the four ports of entry along the two borders for each year. A potential problem is immediately evident from using a sample of inbound trucks to represent the total number of inbound trucks. The purpose of the proxy is to detect annual changes in truckload sizes entering the U.S. Because the Custom districts include many smaller ports of entry, the combined number of inbound trucks at the four ports of entry may not accurately represent the total number of inbound trucks associated with the four Custom districts. If this is the case, the annual changes in truckload sizes could not be determined with this proxy. To address this concern, I compared the number of inbound trucks from the four ports of entry to the total number of inbound trucks from all of the ports of entry within the four Custom districts for the years 1984 to 1993.[14] The simple correlation coefficient between the total number of inbound trucks from all ports of entry and the sample of inbound trucks from the four ports of entry for both borders produced a coefficient of 0.986 for the U.S.-Mexican border and a coefficient of 0.960 for the U.S.-Canadian border. This indicates that the sample of inbound trucks from the four ports of entry closely matches the annual changes in the total number of inbound truckers from the four Custom districts. These data are graphed in Figure 4-6 with the titles "U.S.-Mexican Border" and "U.S.-Canadian Border." The graphs illustrate that, for after 1984 at least, the number of inbound trucks corresponding to the four ports of entry matched the pattern of inbound trucks from the entire sample of Custom districts quite accurately. Thus, the ratio of the sum of the real Custom value of imports by district divided by the sum of the inbound trucks from the four ports of entry should indicate annual changes caused by entry regulations in truckload sizes entering the U.S.

Figure 4-5 plots the truckload sizes over time for both the U.S.-Mexican and U.S.-Canadian borders from 1978 to 1993.

The graph corresponding to the U.S.-Mexican border shows that the truckload sizes entering the U.S. fell sharply in 1980, when the Motor Carrier Act of 1980 opened the U.S.-Mexican border to Mexican

Figure 4-5: Transborder Truckload Sizes

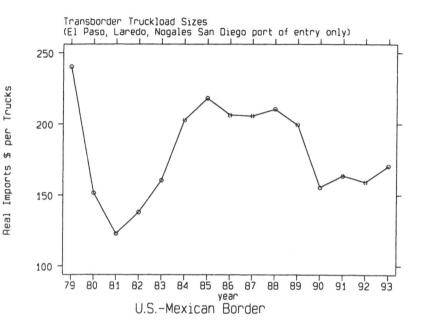

Note: The observation corresponding to 1978 was not included in the U.S.-
Mexican Border graph because data on the number of trucks passing
through the port of San Diego was not available. Including the 1978
without the number of inbound trucks at the San Diego would give the
false impression that truck loads were higher than they actually were in
that year.

Figure 4-5: Transborder Truckload Sizes

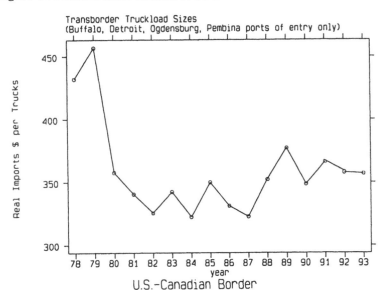

truckers; thus, lowering the fixed cost of transborder trucking for Mexican truckers. Mexican truckers appear to have decreased their load sizes because of this cost reduction. After the Bus Regulatory Reform Act of 1982 and the Motor Carrier Safety Act of 1984 which closed the border and increased the fixed cost of transborder trucking, Mexican truckers appear to have increased their load size entering the U.S. Mexican truckers continued to carry heavy loads until the 1990 U.S. recession, which reduced available cargo to haul and forced load sizes to decrease.

Looking at the graphs corresponding to the U.S.-Canadian border reveals that Canadian truckers' load sizes also fell sharply in 1980, when the Motor Carrier Act of 1980 was passed. Just as in the case for the Mexican truckers, interlining costs were eliminated by MCA and Canadian carriers enjoyed a lower average cost of transborder trucking. Their load sizes remained low until the Motor Vehicle Transportation Act of 1987 which opened the U.S.-Canadian transborder market to U.S. truckers. According to the theoretical model above, Canadian inbound truckload sizes should increase due to the increased uncertainty of full backhauls in the U.S. caused by increased competition and the anti-cabotage laws in the U.S. Since the data on inbound truckers provided by the U.S. Customs does not distinguish the trucks by nationality, one would expect that the increased load size of Canadian fronthauls into the U.S. would be offset by the decreased load sizes of U.S. truckers backhauling from Canada. The increase is moderate at best, but the apparent persistence of this result is interesting. There is a temporary decrease in load size in 1990 but this result is likely due to the 1990 recession making cargo scarce for all truckers.

The pattern of truckload sizes predicted above is consistent with theory, but consideration must be given to the fact that the above graphs are not constructed under ceteris paribus conditions.

4.5 CONSIDERATION OF THE COMPOSITION OF CARGO

Since truckload sizes are measured in real dollars rather than tonnage, the impression that a greater dollar value of cargo means larger cargo loads can be misleading. For example, a truckload of corn is less valuable than a truckload of wrist watches, but their weights may be roughly the same. If the composition of cargo carried by the typical trucker changes from corn to wrist watches, then the real Custom value of imports per inbound truck would incorrectly make it appear that load sizes have increased, when in actuality the cargo has merely changed composition. Thus, the graphs above may be reflecting the compositional changes in cargo rather than changes in tonnage.[15]

To get an idea of the compositional changes that Mexican imports have undergone, refer to Tables 4-2 and 4-3. Table 4-2 shows a time trend of the real dollar value of the top forty imports of 1996 entering the United States from Mexico. The most imported product from Mexico in 1996 was motor cars and other motor vehicles; the fortieth most imported product (in 1994) was iron or steel primary forms & semifinished products. Most of the top 40 imports into the U.S. from Mexico are manufactured goods—primarily automobile parts and appliances. Only five products of the top forty imports can be considered agricultural in nature: vegetables, fruits and nuts, livestock, coffee, and seafood. Nearly all imports have increased in real terms except for the imports of oil (crude and not crude), coffee, and seafood. Automotive vehicles surpassed crude oil as the number one import in 1995, with roughly $20 million worth of goods imported into the U.S.

in 1983, rising to over $6 billion worth of goods imported into the U.S. in 1996. This is a 29,900 percent increase in just thirteen years. Mostly products related to manufacturing, such as electrical equipment and automotive parts, have made the greatest gains. For example, in a twelve year period, imports of automatic data processing machines have increase 16,400 percent, going from $10 million in 1984 to $1.65 billion in 1996.

The change in the rankings of the imported goods into the U.S. are best illustrated in Table 4-3: "Ranking of the 1996 Top 40 U.S. Imports from Mexico 1980 to 1996." Motor cars and other motor vehicles have moved from thirty-first most imported good in 1985 to first in 1996. The category motor vehicle parts for transportation of goods and special purpose vehicles has moved from thirtieth most imported good in 1990 to fifth in 1996. Equipment for distributing electricity has moved from fourteenth most imported good in 1980 to third in 1996. Most of the other manufactured goods have also increased or remained relatively stable over the years, while the five agricultural goods have generally dropped in ranking. The downward trend of the agricultural goods over most of the 1980 to 1996 period, along with the general upward trend in manufactured goods, indicates that Mexican imports to the U.S. have undergone considerable compositional changes. The changes have been toward manufactured goods, which have high dollar value per truckload, and away from agricultural goods, which generally have low dollar value per truckload.

Table 4-4 illustrates the compositional changes of Canadian imports entering the U.S. Table 4-4 shows a time trend of the top forty imports into the U.S. from Canada for 1996. Motor cars and other motor vehicles were the number one most imported good from Canada in 1996, while "Electrical machiner and apparatus, n.e.s." was the fortieth most imported good in 1994. Again, most of the imports are manufactured goods, primarily automotive goods and appliances. A substantial amount of paper products and metals make up the top forty imports. Canadian exports to the U.S. are less reliant on agricultural goods than Mexican exports with only one product, livestock, in the top forty. With the exception of paper and paperboard, natural gas, pulp and waste paper, gold, and live animals, imports have increased in real terms. Motor cars and other vehicles show the greatest increase, with $8.6 billion worth of imports in 1980 to nearly $21 billion in 1996.

Table 4-5 shows the changes in the ranking of the top forty imports to the U.S. from Canada. Only four products have fallen in ranking in 1996 compared to their 1980 level: natural gas, pulp and waste paper, gold, and fertilizer. Of the goods that have increased, parts and accessories of motor vehicles shows the most significant change in ranking from eighteenth in 1980 to fourth in 1996. Overall, compared to Mexico's changes in relative rankings, the changes in Canadian imports seem relatively mild.

Comparing the two sets of Tables, both countries export primarily manufactured goods to the U.S. Canada exports to the U.S. more raw materials and less agricultural goods than Mexico. Mexican imports show the greatest changes in both manufactured and agricultural goods compared to Canada. Relative to Mexico, Canadian exports to the U.S. appear somewhat stable over the seventeen year period. Therefore, the compositional changes of the imported goods from Mexico may have a significant effect on the real custom value of imports per truck entering the U.S. In order to test the validity of the above predictions and quantify the changes in load sizes of the transborder truckers under different regulatory regimes, the compositional changes in the goods imported into the U.S. must be considered.

4.6 ESTIMATES OF THE CHANGE IN TRUCKLOAD SIZES

To estimate the percent change in truckload sizes, controlling for cargo composition changes, the real Custom value of imports per inbound truck will be regressed on a control variable representing compositional changes in imports, the gross domestic product of the United States, and a vector of dummy variables representing the periods of change in entry regulations. The variable used to control for compositional changes in transborder shipments will be the percent of manufactured exports from either Mexico or Canada. The control variable will be called *%mfg*. Also, the annual real gross domestic product of the U.S. will be used in the regression to control for changes in the U.S. economy that may have caused changes in the level of imports entering the U.S. Since the 1980 Motor Carrier Act, the two borders have undergone divergent regulatory regime paths. The U.S.-Mexican border has undergone increased truck entry regulations while the U.S.-Canadian border has undergone increasing truck entry deregulation. The vector of regulatory fixed effects will be a vector of dummy variables taking on the value of one for the time periods when the entry barriers were inactive or removed. The coefficients on the dummy variables will give the estimates of the deviation from the intercept terms from each regression. The intercept term of the regression for the U.S.-Mexican border represents the periods of truck entry deregulation, while the intercept term of the regression for the U.S.-Canadian border will represent the periods of regulated truck entry. Once the coefficients on the dummy variables are estimated the percentage change in load sizes will be calculated and reported.

The model used to estimate the average load size is:

$$loadsize_t = \beta_0\, rGDP_t + \beta_1\, \%\, mfg_t + \sum_{i=2} \beta_i\, (\,fixed\ effects\,) + \varepsilon_t$$

The *fixed effects* for the U.S.-Canadian border are defined as:

$c80\_93 =$ 1 for the years 1980-1993 (the years of Motor Carrier Act), and 0 otherwise.

$c87\_93 =$ 1 for the years 1987-1993 (the years of Motor Vehicle Transportation Act), and 0 otherwise.

The *fixed effects* for the U.S.-Mexican border are defined as:

$m78\_79 =$ 1 for the years 1978-1979 (period of unilateral entry barriers), and 0 otherwise.

$m82\_93 =$ 1 for the years 1982-1993 (the years of Bus Regulatory Reform Act), and 0 otherwise.

$m84\_93 =$ 1 for the years 1984-1993 (the years of Motor Carrier Safety Act), and 0 otherwise.

The OLS regression results, corrected for first order serial correlation by the Cochrane-Orcutt procedure, are listed in Table 4-1.[16]

The pattern of inbound truckload sizes predicted by theory and supported by the graphs in Figure 4-5 above has not dramatically changed even when controlling for compositional changes in imports and fluctuations in the U.S. economy. The results for the U.S.-Mexican border show that prior to deregulating truck entry (represented by *m78_79*) into the U.S. by the Motor Carrier Act of 1980 (the intercept term), Mexican inbound truckload sizes were 21.87 percent higher just prior to opening the U.S. side of the U.S.-Mexican border. This suggests that after the U.S. allowed Mexican truckers easier access to the U.S. transborder trucking market, Mexican inbound truckload sizes fell by nearly 22 percent. According to theory, this result is due to the avoidance of fixed costs of interlining cargo at the border. The MCA allowed Mexican truckers to single-line shipments to the United States, and thus, the Mexican truckers did not have to interline at the border. The Bus Regulatory Reform Act of 1982 (*m82_93*), which limited Mexican truckers from entering the U.S., increased inbound truckload sizes by 3.04 percent. However, this increase is only significant at a confidence level of 63 percent. This implies that inbound truckload sizes could actually have been the same size as the truckload sizes during the deregulatory period of 1980-1981 (corresponding to the intercept term). The Motor Carrier Safety Act of 1984 (*m84_93*), which restricted nearly all Mexican truckers from entering the U.S., caused inbound truckload sizes to increase by 16.63 percent over the truckload sizes transported into the U.S. during the BRRA period. The combined increases in truckload sizes caused by the two restrictive policies, the BRRA and MCSA, have increased Mexican inbound truckloads by 19.67 percent, which would bring the load sizes back up to nearly the same level as before deregulation in 1980. Theory suggests this result is due to the increase in the fixed cost of interlining at the U.S.-Mexican border. Thus, it appears that the opening of the U.S. side of the U.S.-Mexican border lowered the fixed cost associated with transborder trucking and caused Mexican truckers to decrease their load sizes. The closure of the international border caused fixed costs to increase and Mexican truckers to increase their load sizes destined for the U.S.

The results from the regression for the U.S.-Canadian border shows that the Motor Carrier Act of 1980 (*c80-93*), which allowed Canadian truckers easier access to the U.S. transborder market, decreased Canadian inbound truckload sizes by 18.88 percent over the truckload sizes hauled during 1978 and 1979 (represented by the intercept term), a period of unilaterally high entry barriers. Theory suggests that this result is due to the truckers experiencing lower fixed cost from single-lining cargo. The results also show that the Motor Vehicle Transportation Act of 1987 (*c87_93*), which deregulated entry on the Canadian side of the border, caused inbound truckloads (both Canadian and U.S.) into the United States to decrease by only

Table 4-1: Regression Results

| | U.S.-Mexican Border | | | U.S.-Canadian Border | |
variable	coefficients	% change	variable	coefficients	% change
rGDP	-.1059041	—	rGDP	.1184295	—
	(-10.428)			(3.027)	
%mfg	2.015632	—	%mfg	-9.672443	—
	(5.832)			(-3.097)	
m78_79	108.0007	21.87	c80_93	-137.9509	-18.88
	(6.939)			(-11.604)	
m82_93	14.99321	3.04	c87_93	-12.103	-17.23
	(0.971)			(-0.793)	
m84_93	82.11393	19.66	constant	730.4549	—
	(9.066)		(regulation)	(6.582)	
constant	493.8538	—			
(deregulation)	(12.765)				

t-statistics are in parentheses

1.66 percent after 1987. However, the confidence level of this result is only 34 percent. This implies that inbound truckload sizes may have actually been equal to the truckload sizes during the MCA deregulatory period after 1980. This is an understandable result. Before MVTA, only Canadian truckers transported cargo from Canada to the U.S. After the U.S.-Canadian border became unilaterally deregulated by MVTA, both U.S. and Canadian trucks could ship cargo into the U.S. The number of inbound trucks used to calculate the average load size used here is both U.S. and Canadian trucks after this deregulatory period. Thus, Canadian truckers' heavier fronthaul loads entering the U.S. may be offset by the lighter backhaul loads from Canada to the U.S. by U.S. truckers. With this considered, the effect of MVTA and MCA together, accepting the coefficient estimate as being correct, caused inbound truckload sizes to decrease by 17.23 percent after 1987.

4.7 CONCLUSION

The regression results provide evidence that regulations forcing interlining of transborder shipments at the border increase the fixed cost of transborder trucking. When entry barriers are asymmetrically relaxed and foreign truckers are allowed to cross the border into the U.S. but U.S. truckers are prohibited from crossing the border, foreign truckers decrease their fronthaul loads into the U.S. The foreign truckers lighten their fronthaul loads because they perceive a higher probability of full backhaul loads in the U.S. Because foreign truckers have free access to the U.S., foreign truckers can avoid the fixed cost of interlining at the border that U.S. truckers must incur. In essence, foreign truckers have a cost advantage over U.S. truckers in transborder movements which in turn weakens the effectiveness of anti-cabotage laws in preventing foreign truckers from finding backhaul loads in the U.S. The more efficient foreign truckers can out-compete the higher cost U.S. truckers for cargo, making the likelihood of full backhauls in the U.S. more probable. With a high probability of full backhaul loads in the U.S., lighter fronthaul loads carried into the U.S. are possible. Eventually, the asymmetric entry barriers will allow foreign truckers to increase their presence in the market by displacing U.S. transborder truckers. This implies that the anti-cabotage laws in place in the U.S. would be

Table 4- 2. Real Custom Value of the 1996 Top 40 U.S. Imports from Mexico 1980 to 1996 ($ billions)

	1980	1981	1982	1983	1984	1985	1986	1987	1988	1989	1990	1991	1992	1993	1994	1995	1996
Motor cars and oth motor vehicles	n/a	0.00	0.00	0.02	0.05	0.65	0.61	1.57	1.57	1.35	2.35	2.72	2.59	2.94	3.55	5.00	6.46
Crude oil from petroleum or bituminous minerals.	13.53	12.02	14.83	13.64	10.95	5.06	4.78	4.81	3.54	4.61	5.24	4.59	4.36	4.04	4.18	4.66	5.20
Equipment for distributing electricity, n.e.s.	0.36	0.49	0.46	0.57	0.74	1.14	1.07	0.69	1.50	1.77	1.76	1.78	2.01	2.18	2.67	2.87	3.09
Telecommunications equipment, n.e.s. & pts, n.e.s. .	0.96	0.78	0.79	0.80	0.81	0.78	0.74	0.67	0.67	1.15	1.19	1.22	1.23	1.29	1.81	2.22	2.56
Motor vehicles for transpt of gds & spec pur vehs	n/a	0.00	0.00	0.00	0.07	0.23	0.22	0.12	0.00	0.14	0.25	0.21	0.44	0.52	0.58	1.52	2.50
Parts and accessories of motor vehicles, ect.	0.41	0.42	0.42	0.51	0.68	0.78	0.74	0.88	1.16	1.23	1.33	1.52	1.97	2.24	2.14	2.07	2.27
Television receivers	0.70	0.76	0.72	0.73	0.65	0.79	0.75	0.84	1.19	0.98	1.00	1.02	1.28	1.51	2.04	2.14	2.25
Special transactions & commod not classif by knd	0.59	0.68	0.69	0.52	0.53	0.76	0.72	0.84	1.01	1.17	1.10	1.15	1.17	1.27	1.44	1.78	1.83
Automatic data process machs & units thereof	n/a	n/a	n/a	0.00	0.01	0.06	0.06	0.20	0.31	0.53	0.44	0.40	0.46	0.46	0.84	0.96	1.65
Internal combust piston engs, and pts, n.e.s.	0.10	0.16	0.42	0.83	0.93	1.23	1.16	1.18	1.11	0.94	0.75	0.73	0.89	0.96	1.41	1.61	1.60
Elecrcl apparat for switchg or protectg elec circ	0.42	0.47	0.48	0.51	0.58	0.64	0.61	0.69	0.88	0.99	1.05	1.04	1.08	1.28	1.55	1.56	1.56
Electrical machinery and apparatus, n.e.s. .	0.43	0.39	0.34	0.39	0.50	0.58	0.55	0.67	0.74	0.83	0.81	0.85	0.90	0.92	1.15	1.28	1.31
Furniture & pts; bedding, mattreses, etc.	0.13	0.13	0.12	0.17	0.23	0.36	0.34	0.41	0.56	0.61	0.63	0.69	0.78	0.84	1.00	1.03	1.24
Articles of apparel of textile fabrics nes	n/a	n/a	n/a	n/a	n/a	0.12	0.11	0.14	0.15	0.14	0.26	0.31	0.41	0.49	0.64	0.95	1.13
Vegs fr, chld, froz; roots, tubers etc fresh, drie	0.71	0.90	0.80	0.80	0.71	0.94	0.89	0.66	0.62	0.79	0.99	0.85	0.72	0.90	0.90	1.03	1.13
Electric power machineery, and parts thereof	0.21	0.22	0.22	0.27	0.37	0.41	0.38	0.44	0.51	0.42	0.47	0.51	0.53	0.65	0.63	0.79	0.97
Radio broadcast receivers .	0.00	0.02	0.08	0.36	0.43	0.60	0.57	0.80	1.14	0.83	0.67	0.66	0.63	0.62	0.82	0.92	0.91
Thermionic, cold cathode, photocathode valves .	0.32	0.35	0.32	0.31	0.38	0.42	0.40	0.42	0.40	0.50	0.51	0.47	0.47	0.57	0.70	0.82	0.83
Men's or boy's coats, jackets etc, text, not knit .	n/a	n/a	n/a	n/a	n/a	0.19	0.18	0.21	0.24	0.25	0.20	0.25	0.32	0.37	0.44	0.65	0.82

Rotating electric plant and parts thereof, n.e.s.	0.13	0.17	0.16	0.17	0.20	0.26	0.24	0.27	0.32	0.36	0.33	0.38	0.48	0.53	0.65	0.73	0.81
Measuring/checking/analyzing & contr inst&appt	0.18	0.18	0.12	0.14	0.18	0.20	0.19	0.21	0.25	0.30	0.29	0.37	0.49	0.55	0.58	n/a	n/a
Parts etc for office mach & auto data process mach	0.18	0.21	0.25	0.31	0.42	0.38	0.36	0.42	0.48	0.33	0.31	0.32	0.45	0.49	0.57	n/a	n/a
Househld type elec & nonelec equipment, n.e.s.	n/a	n/a	0.13	0.13	0.12	0.14	0.13	0.17	0.21	0.31	0.35	0.41	0.48	0.53	0.52	n/a	n/a
Pumps, air or other gas compressors and fans	0.00	0.00	0.00	0.00	0.00	0.00	0.00	0.00	0.00	0.00	0.11	0.11	0.14	0.17	0.48	n/a	n/a
Meters and counters, nes .	0.00	0.00	0.00	0.00	0.00	0.00	0.00	0.00	0.00	0.00	0.01	0.02	0.04	0.21	0.48	n/a	n/a
Manufactures of base metal, n.e.s .	0.11	0.11	0.12	0.12	0.14	0.17	0.16	0.20	0.23	0.35	0.32	0.32	0.34	0.37	0.44	n/a	n/a
Baby carriages, toys, games and sporting goods	0.11	0.10	0.12	0.16	0.15	0.17	0.16	0.16	0.24	0.29	0.27	0.29	0.29	0.34	0.42	n/a	n/a
Heatng & coolng equipmnt and pts thereof, n.e.s.	n/a	n/a	0.00	0.00	0.03	0.10	0.09	0.16	0.21	0.23	0.17	0.23	0.28	0.30	0.40	n/a	n/a
Fruit, nuts (not including oil nuts) fresh or drie .	0.20	0.17	0.19	0.19	0.17	0.23	0.21	0.25	0.24	0.26	0.31	0.40	0.45	0.38	0.36	n/a	n/a
Taps, cocks, values & sim appliances	n/a	n/a	n/a	n/a	n/a	n/a	n/a	n/a	n/a	n/a	0.18	0.19	0.24	0.31	0.35	n/a	n/a
Women/girls coats, capes etc, tex fabric, not knit .	n/a	n/a	n/a	n/a	n/a	0.10	0.09	0.14	0.15	0.16	0.17	0.22	0.27	0.26	0.35	n/a	n/a
Live animals other than animals of division 03 .	0.11	0.14	0.22	0.25	0.16	0.42	0.40	0.34	0.32	0.33	0.46	0.38	0.34	0.41	0.32	n/a	n/a
Inst & appls, nes, for medical, dental etc purpose .	n/a	n/a	n/a	n/a	0.05	0.12	0.11	0.15	0.25	0.23	0.26	0.29	0.29	0.29	0.31	n/a	n/a
Estimate of low valued imports transactions	n/a	n/a	n/a	0.22	0.22	0.13	0.12	0.17	0.18	0.24	0.32	0.32	0.32	0.34	0.31	n/a	n/a
Coffee and coffee substitutes	0.70	0.50	0.51	0.49	0.52	0.87	0.82	0.53	0.37	0.58	0.37	0.35	0.25	0.24	0.30	n/a	n/a
Oil (not crude) from petrol & bitum minerals etc. .	0.10	0.16	0.42	0.83	0.93	0.62	0.59	0.36	0.44	0.24	0.33	0.23	0.28	0.53	0.29	n/a	n/a
Musical instruments and parts, records, tapes etc	n/a	n/a	n/a	n/a	0.06	0.09	0.09	0.12	0.18	0.19	0.20	0.22	0.22	0.24	0.29	n/a	n/a
Alcoholic beverages	0.15	0.17	0.15	0.13	0.14	0.25	0.24	0.35	0.28	0.24	0.25	0.22	0.24	0.26	0.27	n/a	n/a
Crustacean etc frsh, ch, fz, drd, salted, etc .	0.73	0.58	0.72	0.69	0.61	0.51	0.48	0.56	0.40	0.38	0.23	0.22	0.17	0.22	0.26	n/a	n/a
Iron or steel primary forms & semifinished products .	0.00	0.00	0.00	0.00	0.00	0.00	0.00	0.00	0.00	0.00	0.06	0.05	0.02	0.08	0.26	n/a	n/a

n/a   data not available.

source: U.S. Department of Commerce, International Trade Administration, *U.S. Foreign Trade Highlights*

Table 4-3. Ranking of the 1996 Top 40 U.S. Imports from Mexico 1980 to 1996 (by Custom value)

	1980	1981	1982	1983	1984	1985	1986	1987	1988	1989	1990	1991	1992	1993	1994	1995	1996
Motor cars and oth motor vehicles.	n/a	n/a	n/a	n/a	n/a	31	10	2	2	3	2	2	2	2	2	1	1
Crude oil from petroleum or bituminous minerals .	1	1	1	1	1	1	1	1	1	1	1	1	1	1	1	2	2
Equipment for distributing electricity, n.e.s.	14	10	12	9	5	4	3	3	3	2	3	3	3	4	3	3	3
Telecommunications equipment, n.e.s. & pts, n.e.s.	3	4	4	6	4	6	5	10	11	6	5	5	6	6	6	4	4
Motor vehicles for transpt of gds & spec pur vehs .	n/a	n/a	n/a	n/a	n/a	n/a	n/a	n/a	n/a	n/a	30	36	22	20	20	10	5
Parts and accessories of motor vehicles, ect.	13	13	14	12	7	7	8	5	5	4	4	4	4	3	4	6	6
Television receivers	7	5	6	7	8	10	6	7	4	8	8	8	5	5	5	5	7
Special transactions & commod not classif by kind	9	6	7	7	11	8	9	6	8	5	6	6	7	8	8	7	8
Automatic data process machs & units thereof	n/a	n/a	n/a	n/a	n/a	n/a	n/a	31	23	15	17	17	19	23	13	14	9
Internal combust piston engs, and pts, n.e.s.	31	25	13	4	3	2	2	4	7	9	11	11	10	9	9	8	10
Elecricl apparat for switchg or protectg elec circ	12	12	11	13	10	11	11	9	9	7	7	7	8	7	7	9	11
Electrical machinery and apparatus, n.e.s	11	15	16	16	13	14	14	11	10	11	10	9	9	10	10	11	12
Furniture & pts; bedding, mattresses, etc.	28	29	27	25	22	22	21	18	13	13	13	12	11	12	11	13	13
Articles of apparel of textile fabrics nes .	n/a	n/a	n/a	n/a	n/a	n/a	n/a	n/a	n/a	n/a	29	26	23	21	17	15	14
Vegs fr, chld, froz; roots, tubers etc fresh, drie .	5	3	3	5	6	5	4	12	12	12	9	10	12	11	12	12	15
Electric power machinery and apparatus, n.e.s.	17	17	20	20	20	20	14	15	14	17	15	14	14	13	18	18	16
Radio broadcast receivers .	35	33	32	17	16	9	13	8	6	10	12	13	13	14	14	16	17
Thermionic, cold cathode, photocathode valves etc.	15	16	17	18	18	17	17	16	18	16	14	15	18	15	15	17	18
Men's or boy's coats, jackets etc, text, not knit	n/a	22	24	26	24	23	n/a	24	22	29	35	29	27	26	26	20	19
Rotating electric plant and parts thereof, n.e.s.	25	22	24	26	24	23	24	24	22	20	20	20	16	18	16	19	20
Measuring/checking/analyzing & contr inst&appt .	22	20	29	27	25	29	30	28	27	25	26	21	15	16	19	n/a	n/a

Commodity																	
Parts etc for office mach & auto data process mach	21	19	18	19	17	15	20	17	15	23	24	23	21	22	21	n/a	n/a
Household type elec & nonelec equipment, n.e.s.	n/a	n/a	n/a	n/a	n/a	n/a	n/a	33	33	24	19	16	17	17	22	n/a	n/a
Pumps, air or other gas compressors and fans	n/a	n/a	n/a	n/a	n/a	n/a	n/a	n/a	n/a	n/a	n/a	n/a	n/a	n/a	23	n/a	n/a
Meters and counters, nes.	n/a	n/a	n/a	n/a	n/a	n/a	n/a	n/a	n/a	n/a	n/a	n/a	n/a	n/a	24	n/a	n/a
Manufactures of base metal, n.e.s	30	30	26	30	31	33	33	30	32	21	23	24	25	27	25	n/a	n/a
Baby carriages, toys, games and sporting goods	29	31	28	28	30	32	34	38	30	26	22	28	29	30	27	n/a	n/a
Heating & coolng equipmnt and pts thereof, n.e.s.	n/a	n/a	n/a	n/a	n/a	n/a	n/a	39	n/a	n/a	n/a	31	31	32	28	n/a	n/a
Fruit, nuts (not including oil nuts) fresh or drie	18	21	21	23	28	26	27	26	31	28	25	18	20	25	29	n/a	n/a
Taps, cocks, valves & sim appliances	n/a	n/a	n/a	n/a	n/a	n/a	n/a	n/a	n/a	n/a	38	38	35	31	30	n/a	n/a
Women/girls coats, capes etc, tex fabric, not knit	n/a	n/a	n/a	n/a	n/a	n/a	n/a	29	29	39	n/a	32	32	34	31	n/a	n/a
Live animals other than animals of division 03	19	27	19	21	29	27	18	22	21	22	16	19	24	24	32	n/a	n/a
Inst & appls, nes, for medical, dental etc purpose	n/a	n/a	n/a	n/a	n/a	n/a	n/a	40	36	35	28	27	28	33	33	n/a	n/a
Estimate of low valued imports transactions	n/a	n/a	n/a	n/a	n/a	n/a	n/a	n/a	n/a	30	22	25	26	29	34	n/a	n/a
Coffee and coffee substitutes	6	11	8	14	12	12	22	14	19	14	18	22	33	37	35	n/a	n/a
Oil (not crude) from petrol & bitum minerals etc.	16	7	9	2	2	3	12	24	16	32	21	30	30	19	36	n/a	n/a
Musical instruments and parts, records, tapes etc	n/a	n/a	n/a	n/a	n/a	n/a	n/a	n/a	38	37	34	33	33	36	37	n/a	n/a
Alcoholic beverages	23	24	n/a	29	33	30	25	21	25	31	31	34	34	35	38	n/a	n/a
Crustacean etc frsh, ch, fz, drd, salted, etc	4	8	n/a	8	9	13	16	13	17	18	32	35	n/a	39	39	n/a	n/a
Iron or steel primary forms & simifinished products	n/a	n/a	n/a	n/a	n/a	n/a	n/a	n/a	n/a	n/a	n/a	n/a	n/a	n/a	40	n/a	n/a

n/a   data not available.

source: U.S. Department of Commerce, International Trade Administration, *U.S. Foreign Trade Highlights.*

Table 4-4. Real Custom Value of the 1996 Top 40 U.S. Imports from Canada 1980 to 1996 ($ billions)

	1980	1981	1982	1983	1984	1985	1986	1987	1988	1989	1990	1991	1992	1993	1994	1995	1996
Motor cars and oth motor vehicles.	8.67	8.67	11.24	12.98	16.24	16.75	17.73	13.65	16.50	14.88	14.96	14.92	14.48	17.50	20.41	21.38	20.89
Crude oil from petroleum or bituminous minerals.	4.95	3.87	4.30	4.81	5.65	6.63	4.39	4.51	3.71	3.60	4.80	4.90	4.82	4.76	4.42	5.28	6.02
Paper and paperboard.	6.93	6.70	6.32	6.00	6.47	6.29	6.54	6.65	6.96	6.90	6.58	6.16	5.58	5.46	5.21	6.84	6.00
Parts and accessories of motor vehicles, ect. .	3.94	4.09	4.38	5.82	7.16	8.18	8.21	7.73	8.03	7.60	6.20	5.20	5.52	5.84	5.92	5.61	5.65
Wood, simply worked and railway sleepers of wood.	4.62	3.91	3.27	4.76	4.44	4.37	4.48	4.14	3.68	3.52	2.94	2.78	3.45	4.69	5.25	4.49	5.35
Special transactions & commod not classif by knd.	3.17	3.28	3.55	3.47	3.52	3.60	3.84	3.32	3.21	3.63	4.08	3.91	4.06	4.11	4.86	5.13	5.27
Motor vehicles for transpt of gds & spec pur vehs.	3.06	4.01	5.06	4.87	5.88	5.37	4.56	4.96	5.27	6.31	6.55	6.32	7.52	7.22	6.05	5.66	5.19
Natural gas, whether or not liquefied	n/a	n/a	n/a	n/a	n/a	4.18	2.72	2.23	2.19	1.95	2.19	2.46	2.73	3.09	3.51	2.79	3.20
Aluminum.	1.53	1.60	1.14	1.51	1.73	1.34	1.84	2.06	2.50	2.40	1.95	1.86	1.84	1.92	2.51	2.95	2.54
Furniture & pts; bedding, mattresses, etc.	0.76	0.73	0.75	0.94	1.18	1.33	1.50	1.36	1.40	1.35	1.12	1.12	1.27	1.48	1.82	2.09	2.37
Telecommunications equipment, n.e.s. & pts.	0.57	0.59	0.63	0.63	0.91	0.86	0.77	0.72	0.90	0.90	0.96	1.02	1.09	1.21	1.39	1.65	2.19
Oil (not crude) from petrol & bitum minerals etc.	1.38	2.08	1.65	2.25	2.26	2.46	1.49	1.37	1.67	1.82	2.20	2.00	1.62	1.60	1.42	1.46	2.05
Parts etc for office mach & auto data process mach	0.37	0.41	0.40	0.44	0.68	0.31	0.59	0.50	0.53	1.43	0.14	1.61	1.49	1.41	1.99	2.56	2.03
Internal combust piston engs, and pts, n.e.s..	0.68	1.03	1.29	1.84	2.23	0.25	2.20	2.15	2.34	2.33	1.91	1.37	1.41	1.66	1.59	1.45	1.97
Pulp and waste paper .	3.78	3.41	2.72	2.47	2.73	2.08	2.14	2.48	2.79	3.08	2.77	1.97	1.79	1.55	1.79	2.77	1.81
Aircraft & associated equipmt; spccrft vet; & pts	1.14	1.45	1.45	1.23	1.43	1.52	1.82	1.61	1.60	1.42	1.92	2.15	1.71	1.21	1.45	1.39	1.79
Thermionic, cold cathode, photocathode valves	n/a	n/a	0.27	0.32	0.60	0.52	0.61	0.84	0.93	1.06	1.12	1.52	1.75	1.32	1.24	1.50	1.77
Road motor vehicles, n.e.s. .	0.54	0.76	0.58	0.56	0.69	0.70	0.65	0.90	0.79	0.67	0.60	0.56	0.60	0.86	1.52	1.81	1.70
Gold, nonmonetary (excluding ores & cncentrates)	2.76	2.60	2.15	1.73	2.52	2.32	3.64	1.15	0.86	1.03	0.47	1.22	1.24	1.52	1.36	1.14	1.37
Estimate of low valued imports transactions .	n/a	0.10	0.10	0.16	0.19	0.63	0.64	0.74	0.81	0.83	0.95	0.93	0.90	0.96	1.13	1.23	1.25

Nonelectric parts & accessories of machry nes	0.00	0.55	0.49	0.50	0.61	0.58	0.59	0.52	n/a	n/a	0.25	0.30	0.28	0.38	1.03	n/a	n/a
Automatic data process machs & units thereof	0.50	0.55	0.55	0.55	0.62	n/a	0.59	0.99	0.94	0.48	0.57	0.78	0.84	0.88	0.96	n/a	n/a
Veneers, plywood, particles bd, oth worked wood nes	n/a	n/a	n/a	n/a	n/a	n/a	n/a	n/a	0.39	0.45	0.40	0.35	0.54	0.71	0.89	n/a	n/a
Manufactures of base metal, n.e.s.	0.59	0.64	0.58	0.67	0.88	0.92	1.00	0.99	1.02	0.90	0.80	0.69	0.69	0.76	0.88	n/a	n/a
Electric current	n/a	n/a	n/a	n/a	n/a	0.00	0.00	0.00	0.00	0.64	0.50	0.51	0.59	0.63	0.86	n/a	n/a
Live animals other than animals of division 03	0.52	0.40	0.53	0.51	0.64	0.55	0.40	0.36	0.59	0.61	0.77	0.80	1.02	1.00	0.84	n/a	n/a
Electricl apparat for switchg or protectg elec circ	n/a	n/a	n/a	n/a	n/a	0.37	0.39	0.42	0.48	0.70	1.56	1.46	0.85	0.79	0.83	n/a	n/a
Rubber tires, inter treads, tire flaps & inn tubes	0.51	0.53	0.70	0.69	0.82	0.70	0.78	0.71	0.55	0.67	0.67	0.72	0.76	0.79	0.80	n/a	n/a
Fertilizers (except crude of group 272)	2.13	2.06	1.52	1.36	1.39	1.00	0.85	0.77	0.88	0.81	0.82	0.76	0.76	0.76	0.79	n/a	n/a
Articles, nes of Plastics	n/a	n/a	n/a	n/a	n/a	0.38	0.49	0.54	0.62	0.59	0.56	0.50	0.55	0.63	0.78	n/a	n/a
Engs and motors, nonelect & pts, n.e.s.	n/a	n/a	n/a	n/a	n/a	0.54	0.58	0.59	0.63	0.65	0.77	0.70	0.68	0.78	0.76	n/a	n/a
Copper	n/a	n/a	n/a	0.39	0.59	0.39	0.53	0.59	0.71	0.73	0.61	0.59	0.62	0.57	0.72	n/a	n/a
Railway vehicles & associated equipment	n/a	n/a	n/a	n/a	n/a	0.12	0.30	0.30	0.23	0.65	0.54	0.44	0.40	0.42	0.72	n/a	n/a
Polymers of ethylene, in primary forms	n/a	n/a	n/a	n/a	n/a	n/a	n/a	n/a	n/a	0.39	0.40	0.37	0.42	0.48	0.64	n/a	n/a
Measuring/checking/analyzing & contr inst&appt	n/a	n/a	n/a	n/a	n/a	n/a	0.56	0.56	0.46	0.46	0.50	0.53	0.52	0.51	0.59	n/a	n/a
Machry etc specializd for particulr industries nes	0.31	0.38	0.42	0.47	0.87	0.41	0.37	0.49	0.58	0.51	0.39	0.35	0.38	0.43	0.58	n/a	n/a
Iron & steel tubes, pipes & hol profiles, fittings	n/a	n/a	n/a	n/a	n/a	0.52	0.55	0.51	0.54	0.48	0.42	0.39	0.46	0.54	0.55	n/a	n/a
Paper & paperboard, cut to size or shape, articles	n/a	n/a	n/a	n/a	n/a	n/a	n/a	n/a	n/a	n/a	0.27	0.29	0.38	0.42	0.53	n/a	n/a
Mechanical handling equipmt, & pts thereof, n.e.s.	n/a	n/a	n/a	n/a	n/a	n/a	n/a	n/a	n/a	n/a	0.35	0.30	0.32	0.39	0.50	n/a	n/a
Electrical machinery and apparatus, n.e.s.	n/a	n/a	n/a	n/a	n/a	n/a	n/a	n/a	n/a	n/a	0.36	0.34	0.41	0.41	0.49	n/a	n/a

n/a   data not available.

source: U.S. Department of Commerce, International Trade Administration, *U.S. Foreign Trade Highlights*.

Table 4- 5. Ranking of the 1996 Top 40 U.S. Imports from Canada 1980 to 1996 (by Custom value)

	1980	1981	1982	1983	1984	1985	1986	1987	1988	1989	1990	1991	1992	1993	1994	1995	1996
Motor cars and oth motor vehicles.	2	2	1	1	1	1	1	1	1	1	1	1	1	1	1	1	1
Crude oil from petroleum or bituminous minerals.	4	7	6	6	2	3	6	5	5	6	5	5	5	5	7	5	2
Paper and paperboard.	3	3	3	3	4	4	3	3	2	3	2	3	3	4	5	2	3
Parts and accessories of motor vehicles, ect.	18	25	25	16	20	17	17	17	15	2	4	4	4	3	3	4	4
Wood, simply worked and railway sleepers of wood.	5	6	8	7	7	7	4	6	6	7	7	7	7	6	4	7	5
Special transactions & commod not classif by knd.	8	8	7	8	8	8	9	7	7	5	6	6	6	7	6	6	6
Motor vehicles for transp of gds & spec pur vehs.	9	5	4	5	5	6	5	4	4	4	3	2	2	2	2	3	7
Natural gas, whether or not liquefied	1	1	2	2	3	5	7	8	8	11	10	8	8	8	8	9	8
Aluminum.	12	14	15	13	13	14	12	10	10	9	11	12	9	9	9	8	9
Furniture & pts; bedding, mattreses, etc.	22	24	22	18	16	15	14	14	14	15	16	18	16	14	11	12	10
Telecommunications equipment, n.e.s. & pts.	28	28	26	25	18	20	23	28	22	21	18	19	18	18	17	14	11
Oil (not crude) from petrol & bitum minerals etc.	14	11	11	10	11	9	13	13	12	12	9	10	13	11	16	16	12
Parts etc for office mach & auto data process mach	34	33	34	34	31	31	22	22	24	13	15	13	14	15	10	11	13
Internal combust piston engs, and pts, n.e.s.	24	17	14	11	12	12	15	11	11	10	13	16	15	10	13	17	14
Pulp and waste paper .	7	9	9	9	9	11	10	9	8	8	8	11	10	12	12	10	15
Aircraft & associated equipmt; specerft vet; & pts	17	15	13	15	14	13	11	12	13	14	12	9	12	17	15	18	16
Thermionic, cold cathode, photocathode valves	n/a	n/a	n/a	n/a	n/a	n/a	31	23	21	17	17	14	11	16	19	15	17
Road motor vehicles, n.e.s.	29	23	29	28	30	31	28	20	30	27	29	31	29	22	14	13	18
Gold, nonmonetary (excluding ores & cncentrates)	10	10	10	12	10	10	8	15	26	18	n/a	17	17	13	18	20	19
Estimate of low valued imports transactions	n/a	n/a	n/a	n/a	n/a	30	29	29	27	23	19	20	20	20	20	19	20
Nonelectric parts & accessories of machry nes .	n/a	n/a	n/a	n/a	n/a	n/a	n/a	n/a	n/a	n/a	n/a	n/a	n/a	n/a	21	n/a	n/a

Automatic data process machs & units thereof	32	30	31	30	40	39	40	33	34	n/a	30	23	22	21	22	23	n/a	n/a
Veneers, plywood, particles bd, oth worked wood nes.	n/a	n/a	n/a	n/a	n/a	n/a	n/a	n/a	n/a	n/a	n/a	32	28	28	23	n/a	n/a	n/a
Manufactures of base metal, n.e.s. .	26	24	28	24	21	18	18	18	17	20	22	25	27	26	25	24	n/a	n/a
Electric current .	n/a	n/a	n/a	n/a	n/a	n/a	n/a	n/a	n/a	32	38	33	31	29	30	25	n/a	n/a
Live animals other than animals of division 03	30	34	32	31	38	n/a	n/a	n/a	38	33	23	22	19	19	19	26	n/a	n/a
Electricl apparat for switchg or protectg elec circ	n/a	n/a	n/a	n/a	n/a	n/a	n/a	n/a	n/a	26	28	15	24	24	21	27	n/a	n/a
Rubber tires, inter treads, tire flaps & inn tubes	31	23	23	23	25	24	24	30	39	28	26	25	23	23	24	28	n/a	n/a
Fertilizers (except crude of group 272).	11	12	12	14	15	16	20	24	25	26	28	24	25	27	23	29	n/a	n/a
Articles, nes of Plastics	n/a	n/a	n/a	n/a	n/a	n/a	n/a	n/a	n/a	34	34	31	31	30	31	30	n/a	n/a
Engs and motors, nonelect & pts, n.e.s. .	n/a	n/a	n/a	n/a	n/a	n/a	n/a	35	32	31	28	26	26	25	25	31	n/a	n/a
Copper.	n/a	n/a	n/a	n/a	n/a	n/a	n/a	n/a	n/a	25	34	28	30	31	28	32	n/a	n/a
Railway vehicles & associated equipment.	n/a	n/a	n/a	n/a	n/a	n/a	n/a	n/a	n/a	30	39	38	38	34	n/a	33	n/a	n/a
Polymers of ethylene, in primary forms	n/a	n/a	n/a	n/a	n/a	n/a	n/a	n/a	n/a	34	n/a	n/a	n/a	n/a	39	34	n/a	n/a
Measuring/checking/analyzing & contr inst&appt.	n/a	n/a	n/a	n/a	n/a	n/a	n/a	38	n/a	39	n/a	32	35	32	34	35	n/a	n/a
Machry etc specializd for particulr industries nes .	n/a	n/a	n/a	n/a	n/a	n/a	n/a	n/a	n/a	n/a	n/a	n/a	n/a	40	n/a	36	n/a	n/a
Iron & steel tubes, pipes & hol profiles, fittings	n/a	n/a	n/a	n/a	n/a	n/a	n/a	n/a	n/a	n/a	n/a	37	32	32	37	37	n/a	n/a
Paper & paperboard, cut to size or shape, articles	n/a	n/a	n/a	n/a	n/a	n/a	n/a	n/a	n/a	n/a	n/a	n/a	n/a	n/a	n/a	38	n/a	n/a
Mechanical handling equipmt, & pts thereof, n.e.s.	n/a	n/a	n/a	n/a	n/a	n/a	n/a	n/a	n/a	n/a	n/a	n/a	n/a	n/a	n/a	39	n/a	n/a
Electrical machinery and apparatus, n.e.s. .	n/a	n/a	n/a	n/a	n/a	n/a	n/a	n/a	n/a	n/a	n/a	n/a	n/a	n/a	n/a	40	n/a	n/a

n/a   data not available.

source: U.S. Department of Commerce, International Trade Administration, *U.S. Foreign Trade Highlights.*

Figure 4-6: Total Number of Inbound Trucks by Custom District and Major Ports of Entry

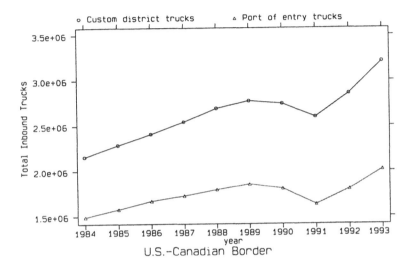

U.S.-Canadian Border

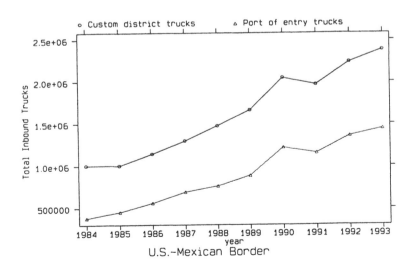

U.S.-Mexican Border

ineffective in preventing foreign truckers from dominating the U.S. transborder market when only the U.S. side of the border is free of entry barriers.

Theory suggests that when both sides of the international border are eventually deregulated, truckload sizes of foreign truckers entering the U.S. will increase as anti-cabotage laws become binding. Prior to unilateral deregulation, the cost advantage of the foreign truckers from not having to interline at the border makes it easier for them to underprice U.S. carriers in obtaining backhaul loads when leaving the U.S. After unilateral deregulation, the backhaul loads are obtained with less certainty. The anti-cabotage laws in the U.S. become binding when U.S. carriers experience a reduction in their interlining fixed cost. When both nations' truckers have no interlining fixed cost, the playing field is level. The anti-cabotage laws restrict the mobility of foreign truckers in the U.S., and with stiffer price competition from U.S. truckers who are not geographically restricted in their own country, cargo for foreign truckers becomes more difficult to obtain. This forces foreign truckers to increase their fronthaul loads to compensate for the expected lighter backhaul loads once inside the U.S. Though theoretically sound, the lack of appropriate data leaves the latter result unsupported. Future research in this area is needed to verify this proposition.

NOTES

1. Recent rulings by Customs officials make it possible for Canadian truckers to make pickups but not deliveries after dropping cargo off in the U.S. Formally, Foreign truckers could only transport a backhaul if and only if the cargo originated along the same route that the trucker used upon entering the U.S.

2. Output is horizontally differentiated because customers located further away from a trucker's terminal pay higher rates. Trucking terminals (and also manufacturing plants) are strategically located to minimize these additional costs. Output is vertically differentiated because consumers perceive quality differences in service. Thus, carriers with high perceived quality output can charge consumers higher rates.

3. In a survey comparing Canadian and U.S. transborder truckload rates, Prentice and Hildebrand (1989, 70) crudely estimate tariff and non-tariff cost to

be .45 cents per pound for Canadian transborder movements, and .38 cents for U.S. transborder movements.

4. The fixed cost does not vary with load sizes. In the case of crossing the U.S.-Mexican border, most of the costs are in terms of wasted time. This is the opportunity cost of transborder trucking. Often truckers will have to wait for hours in line just to reach the actual border crossing (Gooley 1991, 47). The alternative to waiting in line is to transport cargo elsewhere for a fee; hence, the opportunity cost of waiting in line is the loss of revenue from not transporting cargo elsewhere.

5. The average cost curve is U-shaped because, given that the distance is held constant, small loads have high opportunity cost to transport. As load size increases, the opportunity cost of transporting the cargo over a fixed distance decreases. As load size increases, at some point capacity becomes a constraint and loading factors become more costly; thus, average cost increases.

6. The revised expectations may be less than a probability of one, but allowing less than probability one updating would unnecessarily complicate the analysis at this time. All that is important is that backhaul probabilities are revised upward. One could argue that the larger number of new entrants of truckers from country N that replace the truckers from country S create a situation for cut-throat competition between country N truckers competing for backhauls in country S; and thus, weaken the justification for revising upward their expectations. However, because the country N truckers cannot engage in cabotage in country S their mobility between nodes is limited. Because of this the truckers from country N would expect that competition for a backhaul in country S with spatially limited competitors of fellow truckers from country N would be less than what would be in country N where intra-node mobility is not limited. Thus, they would still revise upward their best guess of the probability of obtaining a backhaul in country S.

7. It will be shown later that unilateral deregulation of entry barriers in a symmetric world accompanied by the uncertainty of empty backhauls caused by anti-cabotage laws will create conditions whereby in equilibrium the number of truckers from both countries must be equal.

8. The larger fronthauls are possible because the truckers from country S transport less on their backhauls; thus, allowing the truckers from country N to load $q_1 - \theta q_1$ extra cargo for their fronthauls, where $q_1 - \theta q_1$ is the portion of the backhauls that the truckers from country S do not expect to carry.

9. This assumes an equal amount of goods flowing from country N to country S and from country S to country N.

10. It should be noted that the recent U.S. Customs ruling allowing foreign carriers to make pickups (but no deliveries) on their way out of the U.S. weakens the effect that the anti-cabotage laws have on load sizes. The liberalization of the anti-cabotage laws will essentially cause foreign truckers to revise upward their estimate of the probability of empty backhauls in the U.S.; thus, reducing the necessity to increase fronthauls. In essence, the new ruling will cause the difference in load sizes between fronthauls and backhauls to narrow.

11. There is a strong correlation between dollar value and shipping weight. Using data from the department of transportation (http://www.bts.gov/smart/cat/ztransborder.html), the correlation between shipping weight and value for Mexican imports carried by truck into the U.S. is approximately 84% and for Canadian imports it is 95%.

12. The custom value of imports is generally defined as the price actually paid or payable for merchandise when sold for exportation to the United States, excluding U.S. import duties, freight, insurance and other charges incurred in bringing the merchandise to the U.S.

13. The total annual truck crossings for each port of entry within each Custom district would be a better measure, but U.S. Customs would only provide a consistent time series for a total of eight ports of entry.

14. The U.S. Customs did provide the number of inbound trucks for all ports of entry for the years 1984 to 1993. The labor cost involved in obtaining a consistent time series for all the ports from 1978 to 1983 made the data too costly to obtain.

15. Though there is a high correlation between value and weight, one could argue that the truckers forced to interline at the border would increase the value of the cargo they carry per trip instead of weight. This may be true but only if the trucker is able to choose the cargo to haul. Generally the destination and type of cargo is determined by the shippers. If the trucking industry is sufficiently competitive then truckers will haul whatever type of cargo they can get, limited by what their rigs can carry. The only real control variable available to truckers is the amount of cargo to consolidate per haul.

16. The first order serial correlation coefficient for the U.S.-Mexican regression was -1.0199 with a t-statistic of -5.326. The U.S.-Canadian regression has a first order serial correlation coefficient of -0.5615 with a t-statistic of -2.292 . Without correcting for serial correlation, OLS produced similar results.

CHAPTER 5

Analysis of the
Allocation of Resources

SECTION I: INTERLINING AGENTS AND THEORETICAL MODEL

5.1.1 The Interlining Process

Federal regulations are in place along the U.S.-Mexican border that act as barriers to entry which prevent single-line transport of cargo between the U.S. and Mexico. Until NAFTA opens the border, Mexican truckers are prohibited from transporting cargo directly into the United States, and U.S. truckers are prohibited from transporting cargo directly into Mexico. Despite these barriers to entry, most trade between U.S. and Mexico is transported by truck. International cargo leaving Mexico must be interlined with U.S. truckers at the U.S.-Mexican border before the cargo can be transported into the United States. The cargo exchange must occur within the unregulated commercial zones located around the ports of entry along the U.S. side of the international border.

Today, interlining Mexican shipments at the border is necessary because of regulatory entry barriers, but this has not always been the case. The Motor Carrier Act (MCA) of 1980 briefly allowed Mexican truckers easier access to the U.S.-Mexican transborder market, but this was short-lived. In 1982 with the Bus Regulatory Reform Act (BRRA), the U.S. Congress took measures to limit the Mexican truckers' ability to single-line shipments into the U.S., and in 1984 with the Motor Carrier Safety Act (MCSA) the border was closed to Mexican truckers through safety and liability regulations.

The U.S.-Canadian border has experienced decreased regulation since 1980. Prior to the Motor Carrier Act of 1980, Canadian carriers also had to rely on interlining with U.S. carriers to ensure that their shipments would reach the interior destinations of the U.S. After 1987, with the passing of the Motor Vehicle Transportation Act (MVTA), entry and exit into the U.S. and Canada became relatively free of federal regulations.

Forcing truckers to interline at the border causes resources to be allocated toward the border unnecessarily to facilitate the interlining of cargo. Just as with distortions in the transference of information in a market, economic agents will locate in places and offer services convenient to ameliorate the distortions in the transference of goods between nations. The ports of entry are the most convenient places to locate to assist transborder truckers. Measuring changes in the number of establishments used in the interlining process along the border gives insight into the nature of transborder trucking and provides a means of measuring the movement of resources to border crossings.

This chapter analyzes the resource allocation to the ports of entry along the U.S.-Canadian and U.S.-Mexican borders caused by changes in past transborder trucking regulations. First a theoretical model will be developed followed by a discussion of the data, the variables, and their effects in a regression model. The discussion of the regression results and the estimation of the resources allocated toward the borders will conclude this chapter.

5.1.2 The Supply of Interlining Services

There are three basic types of services used to interline cargo at international borders: transportation arrangement services, transportation services, and warehousing services. Truckers often use freight forwarders or Customs brokers located near ports of entry to arrange pickups and deliveries, prepare the necessary documents for clearing Customs, and assigning tariff rates to the shipments. The demand for the services to weave through the web of tariff classification schemes to get the lowest possible tariff rate for a transborder shipment increases under NAFTA. NAFTA adds to the complexity of tariff classifications. Under NAFTA, numerous goods will be able to be classified under 1,400 different tariff rates (Lasky 1995). Presently, because U.S. truckers are prohibited from entering

Mexico, physically transporting cargo across the Mexican border requires the use of a Mexican cartage or draying company located near ports of entry.[1] These local trucking companies have the authority to transport cargo across the international border. They carry the shipments across the border, go through Customs, and drop the shipments off at terminals were they are picked up by a domestic trucker of that nation who then carries the cargo to its final destination. Delays in crossing the border may induce truckers to store their shipments until crossing is possible. Warehousing establishments can range from small buildings to large refrigerated warehouses. There are other services available to truckers, but these are the primary interlining services that a typical trucker may use to transport its cargo across international boundaries.

The services for interlining international cargo along the borders are nearly perfectly elastic in supply. Firms are relatively small and entry barriers are low.[2] Within the unregulated commercial zones around each port of entry, these interlining agents are relatively free of federal regulations. Special equipment is not necessary to interline cargo. Practically any building can be used as a terminal where the trucks can meet and exchange shipments (large refrigerated warehouses maybe an exception). For example, transportation property brokers require merely a telephone and an office to provide their interlining services (Brown 1984, 12). Also, most establishments are relatively small. Census data shows roughly 80 percent of establishments related to trucking under the Standard Industrial Codes 421, 422 and 473[3] within counties along the northern and southern borders of the U.S. have less than 9 employees.[4] The ratio of employees involved in the arrangement for transportation for freight and cargo (SIC 473) to the total number of employees in Wayne county, MI, (the county containing the port of Detroit—the busiest land-port of entry in the U.S.) shows only 0.2 percent of the employed workforce is involved in this service. The county of El Paso, TX, has 1.0 percent of the county's workforce engaged in this service. As low as these numbers are they may be an exaggeration of the proportion of the workforce in this industry. Surrounding counties add to the labor pool, as does labor from the countries across the borders. Thus, with low barriers to entry and relatively small firms, supply for such services is highly elastic.

Under conditions of low barriers to entry and abundant labor supply, entry into this industry can occur quickly. If, by chance, the demand for interlining services increases, then the rapid entry of firms into the market will erode any chance of obtaining above normal earnings. If the demand for interlining services increases, the market price of interlining services would have a tendency to increase and incumbent firms could earn economic rents. However, entry barriers are low, and new firms will quickly locate around the ports of entry, rapidly increasing the supply of interlining services. The market price for interlining services would fall. Entry into the industry would stop when the market price reaches the original equilibrium market level. The perturbation of the market price would last only for a short period of time. The process would most likely take only a few months to completely work its course. Hence, for longer time frames, the market price for interlining services would appear to be unchanged and the equilibrium quantity of interlining services would be greater. Thus, the low barriers allow rapid entry of firms into this market which makes the supply of interlining services appear nearly perfectly elastic.

5.1.3 Theoretical Means of Measuring the Effects of Regulations

The effects of regulating transborder trucking may be measured by observing the market price and changes in the number of interlining-service establishments located around the ports of entry. Since the interlining service establishments are small, the amount of interlining service provided would be roughly proportional to the number of establishments. An increase in the number of interlining service establishments would be monotonically increasing with the equilibrium amount of interlining services provided at the border. Each establishment would provide a small percentage of the total interlining services produced. Measuring the change in the number of establishments, in response to changes in regulatory regimes, and multiplying that change by an appropriate estimate of the market price of interlining services, will provide a measure of the resources allocated toward the border due to the regulations.

This can be illustrated graphically. Consider Figure 5-1. The NE quadrant illustrates the equilibrium quantity of interlining services. The curve labeled D denotes the demand for interlining services. The curve S denotes the supply of interlining services. Notice that the supply of interlining services is assumed to be perfectly elastic. The SE quadrant represents the monotonic transformation from the equilibrium quantity of interlining services to the number of establishments located along the border, where $0 < \phi \leq 1$. The SW quadrant represents the measure of the resources allocated toward the border.

Figure 5-1: Theoretical Means of Measuring the Effects of Regulations

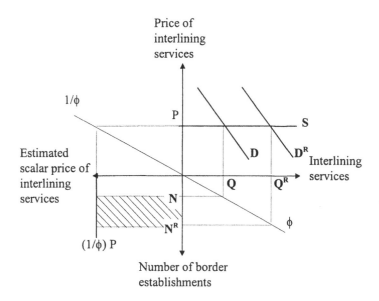

The equilibrium quantity of interlining service, without transborder regulations, is represented by Q in Figure 5-1. Without entry regulations, foreign truckers could single-line cargo into the U.S. and would not have to stop at the border to exchange loads with U.S. truckers. In this case, the equilibrium quantity of interlining services would be low. However, the optimal level of interlining services will be greater than zero. Some services are needed for domestic commerce. In addition, rules against cabotage (point to point transporting of domestic cargo by a foreign carrier) would dictate that the optimal number of establishments would be greater than zero. Since each establishment provides a percent, ϕ, of the total of interlining services produced, Q, the total number of establishments along the border would be $N = \phi Q$.

Now, suppose regulations are imposed on foreign truckers entering the U.S. The regulations force foreign truckers to stop at the border and exchange cargo with U.S. truckers. The forced interlining increases the demand for interlining services at each port of entry. The demand curve for interlining services would shift outward to D^R, and the equilibrium quantity of interlining services would increase to Q^R. Because the supply for interlining services is highly elastic, the equilibrium price of interlining services would be relatively unchanged. The equilibrium number of establishments would increase to N^R.

The resources allocated toward the ports of entry caused by the regulations are represented by the shaded area in the third quadrant. The shaded area is obtained by multiplying an appropriate scalar estimate of the market price of the interlining services by the change in the number of interlining service establishments around the ports of entry along the border, $(1/\phi)P(N^R - N)$, where $(1/\phi)P$ is a scalar estimate of the market price of interlining services. Thus, by estimating the appropriate scalar of the market price of services and the change in the equilibrium number of establishments in response to changes in regulatory regimes, the economic effect of the policy changes can be measured.[5]

If the supply curve of interlining services is not perfectly elastic then the estimate will be exaggerated. However, if not perfectly elastic, the supply curve should be highly elastic and, thus, the estimate will be a good approximation of the dollar amount of resources allocated to the ports of entry.

5.1.4 The Model

In order to model the effects that transborder regulations have on the equilibrium number of interlining service establishments located along the border, the influences of other economic factors must be considered. The goal is to isolate the direct economic effects of the transborder entry regulations on the number of border establishments that locate along the border. If trade barriers are erected by regulations then we would expect the direct effect of the regulations to increase the number of establishments that locate along the border. At the same time, we would expect to see fewer trucks crossing the border. With fewer trucks crossing the border, the demand for interlining services will decrease, and this would reduce the number of establishments located along the border. Therefore, the regulations will have a direct effect that increases the number of establishments along the border and an indirect effect by decreasing the number of trucks crossing the border which decreases the number of interlining service establishments.

Other influences need to be controlled because the number of trucks crossing the border are also affected by the determinants of the level of trade. An increase in trade will increase the number of trucks transporting goods across the border, which will ultimately affect the number of establishments at the border. The economic factors affecting the level of trade are the incomes of the demanders of imports, the tariffs placed on imported goods, and the foreign currency exchange rate.

The regulations and the other economic variables that affect the number of interlining establishments along the border can be presented clearly with a diagram. Consider Figure 5-2.

The number of interlining service establishments that locate along the border is directly influenced by the transborder truck entry regulations and the number of trucks that cross the border. The number of trucks that cross the border is influenced by the transborder truck entry regulations and the level of trade between the U.S. and its contiguous neighbors. The level of trade is affected by exogenous factors such as the real GDP of the countries, tariff rates, and the foreign currency exchange rate. To isolate the direct effects that transborder regulations have on the number of establishments that locate along the border, a recursive-equilibrium model will be constructed based on the above diagram. This model will be used to guide the construction of a detailed regression model to be used to estimate the effects that regulations have on the number of interlining service establishments along the border. The first equation of the model will be a reduced form equation that represents the equilibrium number of establishments along the border. The second equation will represent the equilibrium number of trucks crossing the border. The third equation will represent the equilibrium amount of trade between the countries.

Figure 5-2: Factors Influencing the Number of Border Establishments

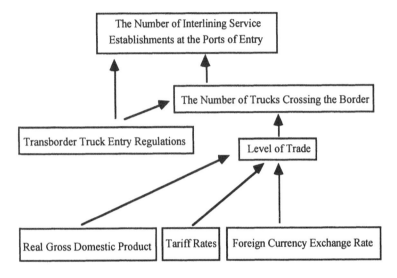

The equilibrium number of establishments along the border is determined by the intersection of the supply and demand for interlining services. The supply of interlining services is $Q^s = k(P)$, where the quantity supplied of interlining services is a perfectly elastic function of the price of the interlining services, P. The demand for interlining services is determined by $Q^d = l(P, trucks, regs)$, where *trucks* is the number of trucks crossing the border and *regs* is a vector of regulation variables; both are exogenous factors. Inverting the supply equation and substituting it into the demand equation gives the quantity demanded as a function of the quantity supplied and the other exogenous factors, $Q^d = l(k^{-1}(Q^s), trucks, regs)$. Noting that the equilibrium quantity of interlining services is $Q^* = Q^s = Q^d$, the new demand equation can be solved for the equilibrium quantity of interlining services in reduced form, $Q^* = f(trucks, regs)$. Understanding that each establishment along the border provides a percentage of the total interlining services produced, the equilibrium number of interlining service establishments is a monotonic transformation of the equilibrium quantity of interlining services: $N^* = \phi Q^*$. This yields equation (1) below.

The equilibrium quantity of trucks crossing the border is determined by the supply and demand for transportation services. The quantity of truck transportation services supplied is determined by a function of the price of truck transportation, $q^s = m(P)$. The quantity of truck transportation demanded is determined by $q^d = k(P, trade, regs)$, where *trade* denotes the quantity of goods shipped across the border and *regs* is a vector of regulation variables, both are exogenous. Substituting the inverted supply equation into the demand equations and solving for the equilibrium quantity of truck transportation service, $q^e = q^s = q^d$, yields $q^e = g(trade, regs)$. The number of trucks crossing the border, q^e_{trucks} represents a percentage, ϕ, of the equilibrium amount of truck transportation service, q^e. An additional variable is included in this equation to account for potential measurement problems. The variable is called *composition*. This variable controls for compositional changes in the types of goods crossing the border when trade is measured by dollar value. Using the number of trucks crossings the border as a percentage of the equilibrium amount of truck transportation service, $q^e_{trucks} = \phi q^e$, yields equation (2).

Equation (3) is determined by the intersection of the supply and demand for traded goods. The quantity supplied of trade is determined as a function of the market price of the goods traded, $q^s_{trade} = s(P)$, where P is the market price. The quantity demanded for the goods traded is $q^q_{trade} = z(P, rGDP, tariff, exchgrte)$, where rGDP is a vector of real gross domestic products of the trading nations, *tariff* is the amount of tariff place on the goods, and *exchgrte* is the foreign currency exchange rate of the trading countries. Inverting the supply equation, substituting it into the quantity demanded equation, and noting that $q^e = q^s = q^d$, the equilibrium amount of trade is determined by $q^e_{trade} = z(rGDP, tariff, exchgrte)$. Also included in this equation will be the variable *composition* noted above to yield equation (3).

$$\overset{+ \quad\quad - \quad\quad\; + \quad\quad\quad + \quad\quad\quad\, ?}{Establishments = f\,(trucks,\ MCA80,\ BRRA82,\ MCSA84,\ MVTA87)} \quad (1)$$

$$\overset{+ \quad\quad\quad + \quad\quad\quad\quad + \quad\quad\quad\; - \quad\quad\quad\; - \quad\quad\quad\; +}{trucks = g\,(trade,\ composition,\ MCA80,\ BRRA82,\ MCSA84,\ MVTA87)} \quad (2)$$

$$\overset{+ \quad\quad\quad + \quad\quad\; - \quad\; + \text{ or } -}{trade = h(composition,\ rGDP,\ tariff,\ exchgrte)} \quad (3)$$

where

Establishments	=	the number of interlining service establishments located around the ports of entry.
trucks	=	number of trucks crossing the international border.
trade	=	amount of trade between countries.
composition	=	composition changes in imports and/or exports.
rGDP	=	a vector of real gross domestic product of each importing country.
tariff	=	tariff rate on traded goods.
exchgrte	=	the foreign currency exchange rate.
MCA80	=	the Motor Carrier Act of 1980.
BRRA82	=	the Bus Regulatory Reform Act of 1982.
MCSA84	=	the Motor Carrier Safety Act of 1984.
MVTA87	=	the Motor Vehicle Transportation Act of 1987.

The predicted signs of each variable are included in equations (1), (2), and (3). Note that the estimated impact of *MCA80, BRRA82, MCSA84* and *MVTA87* from equation (1) are of primary interest. The discussion and the report of the estimates of all other variables will be brief and are included solely for completeness.

In equation (1), the equilibrium number of establishments located around the ports of entry are affected by two factors: the number of trucks that they service and the regulations imposed on these trucks. There should be a positive correlation between the number of trucks serviced and the number of establishments that locate around the ports of entry. Holding all other influences constant, if the number of trucks entering or exiting the U.S. increases, then we would expect the demand for interlining services along the border to increase.

The effect of transborder truck entry regulations on the number of establishments located along the border is more complicated than one would initially think. In general, regulations that restrict truckers from entering a country will increase the demand for interlining services around the ports of entry. Thus, the restrictive policies such as the Bus Regulatory Reform Act (BRRA) of 1982 and the Motor Carrier Safety Act (MCSA) of 1984, which closed the border to Mexican truckers, will increase the number of establishments along the border. The reason is simple: If truckers are forced to interline at the border then the demand for interlining services will increase. Thus, more interlining service establishments will locate along the border where the interlining takes place. The acts of deregulation, such as the Motor Carrier Act (MCA) of 1980, and the Motor Vehicle Transportation Act (MVTA) of 1987, will not necessarily decrease the number of establishments along the border. In fact, it is possible that the number of establishments could increase. Allowing foreign truckers into a country introduces the truckers to another protective regulation: the laws against cabotage.

The laws against cabotage (point to point transporting of cargo entirely within a country by a foreign carrier) may make it economically inviting for more establishments to locate around the ports of entry. First, it should be understood that neither the U.S., Mexico, nor Canada allow cabotage. If the border is regulated against entry, truckers do not face the anti-cabotage constraints because they are restricted from entering the foreign country in the first place. However, when the border is deregulated, the anti-cabotage laws become a binding constraint. For example, in 1980, while Mexico and Canada restricted U.S. trucks from crossing the border, the Motor Carrier Act (MCA) allowed foreign carriers to enter the U.S. to deliver freight. Once the foreign truckers dropped off their freight, they were required to turn around and leave the country with or without cargo. Once in the U.S., if they did not arrange for a load to be picked up at or near their drop-off point, they were forced to return home empty. The rules against cabotage did not allow them to make intermediate pickups and deliveries on their way out of the U.S. in order to avoid empty backhauls. Empty backhauls are very costly.[6] Transportation service establishments located at the ports of entry along the borders offer foreign truckers a convenient place to pick up cargo for the trip back to their home country (Chow 1991, 152-3). Thus, foreign truckers leaving the U.S. could contact one of these establishments and arrange for a load to be picked up at the border to finish the remainder of their homeward journey with a full trailer. In this way, the foreign truckers do not have to travel the whole distance home without cargo. The establishments along the border have incentive to provide such services because they could capture some of the cost savings to the foreign truckers as part of their own profit. So, these establishments, in addition to offering interlining services for international shipments, can consolidate freight to fill the empty backhauls for foreign truckers who would otherwise be leaving the U.S. with empty trailers. Though the foreign truckers would be free of entry barriers and would need less interlining services, they would be more than willing to use the border establishments' services to fill their empty backhauls. It is quite possible that the demand for services to fill empty backhauls would be greater than the reduction in the demand for the interlining services. If this is true, then MCA would increase the number of establishments along the border. However, there is reason to believe that MCA would reduce the number of establishments along the border.

Since MCA allowed foreign truckers into the U.S., once in the U.S., the foreign truckers could single-line shipments back to their home country. The direct-lining of cargo can be a tremendous time-saving service to U.S. shippers. In essence, foreign truckers could offer a service to U.S. shippers that U.S. carriers could not provide. U.S. carriers could not offer this single-line service because they would be forced to interline at the border. Thus, foreign truckers, competing with U.S. truckers for the rights to transport loads of cargo to their home country, could offer single-line services and could easily out-compete U.S. carriers for the cargo to fill their empty backhauls. Thus, empty backhauls would not be a problem for foreign carriers under the Motor Carrier Act. This means there would not be as great a demand for the services to fill empty backhauls at the border. This would most likely make the reduction in the demand for interlining services dominant over increases in demand for services to fill empty backhauls. Therefore, it is hypothesized that MCA will reduce the number of establishments along the border.

The effects that the Motor Vehicle Transportation Act (MVTA) had on the number of establishments that located along the border is less clear. Remember, the MVTA occurred after MCA was in effect. The MVTA opened the Canadian border to U.S. carriers allowing them to conduct single-line services to Canada. This Act in conjunction with MCA stripped away Canadian carriers' monopoly in offering direct-line services to Canada. After MVTA, U.S. carriers could offer the same service as the Canadian carriers. This reduced Canadian carriers' advantage over U.S. carriers in acquiring cargo in the United States to fill their empty backhauls. This would result in an increased likelihood of empty backhauls for Canadians. Thus, the Canadian carriers would demand more services to fill empty backhauls at the border. U.S. truckers hauling cargo directly into Canada, faced with Canadian anti-cabotage laws, would also have demand for services to fill empty backhauls for their return trips to the U.S. The number of transportation service establishments along the border would increase if the reduction in the demand for interlining services, caused by MVTA, is less than the increase in the demand for services to fill empty backhauls caused by the anti-cabotage laws. Therefore, the direction of the change in the number of establishments locating along the border due to MVTA can only be answered empirically.

In equation (2), the number of trucks crossing the international border is a function of the amount of trade that is conducted between the U.S. and its contiguous neighbors, the compositional changes of the cargo carried, and regulations placed on the transborder truckers. The amount of trade between the U.S., Canada, and Mexico should be positively correlated with the number of trucks that cross the border. As more goods (measured in terms of dollar value) are traded between the U.S. and its contiguous neighbors, more trucks will be needed to transport the goods across the borders, ceteris paribus. The compositional changes in the cargo crossing the border should be negatively correlated with the number of trucks crossing the border if the composition change is from low-valued shipments to high-valued shipments. For a given dollar value of trade, if the composition change in cargo is from low-valued shipments (for example, agricultural goods) to high-valued shipments (for example, automobile parts), then we would expect fewer trucks would be needed to transport the higher-valued cargo, ceteris paribus. For example, holding the dollar value of cargo constant, at say $100,000, it takes fewer trucks to transport $100,000 worth of high-valued automobile parts than it takes to transport $100,000 worth of low-valued agricultural goods. Thus, if the composition of cargo changes from low-valued to high-valued goods, it is expected that the number of trucks crossing the border will decrease, ceteris paribus.

The effects of regulations restricting entry to trucks crossing the border should be negatively correlated with the number of trucks crossing the border. Thus, the Bus Regulatory Reform Act and the Motor Carrier Safety Act should be negatively correlated with the number of truck crossings. The deregulation of the U.S. side of the U.S.-Mexican and the U.S.-Canadian borders should increase the number of inbound trucks. Thus, the MCA80 in equation (2) should be positively correlated with the number of trucks crossing the border, ceteris paribus. The deregulation of the Canadian side of the U.S.-

Canadian border by the Motor Vehicle Transportation Act (MVTA) will not have an effect on the number of inbound or outbound trucks. Prior to MVTA, most U.S. freight bound for Canada, carried by U.S. truckers, was interlined at the border. For each shipment carried by a U.S. trucker, a Canadian carrier would have to cross the border and interline with a U.S. trucker. Thus, most inbound and outbound truck movements would be Canadian. After the MVTA, U.S. truckers could direct-line cargo into Canada. The inbound and outbound movements would then be by both U.S. and Canadian trucks. In general, the number of inbound and outbound trucks would be unchanged. Therefore, it is expected that an increase in trade between the U.S. and its neighbors, and deregulatory policy regimes, with the exception of the Motor Vehicle Transportation Act, will increase the number of trucks crossing the border. The MVTA is not expected to affect the number of inbound or outbound trucks. However, compositional changes from low-valued to high-valued shipments, and increases in entry regulations, should decrease the number of trucks crossing the border, ceteris paribus.

In equation (3), the equilibrium level of trade between the U.S. and its contiguous neighbors is a function of the real gross domestic products of the three importing countries, the compositional changes in the goods traded, the tariff rates on the traded goods, and the foreign currency exchange rate. A positive correlation should exist between the real gross domestic products and the level of trade among the three countries. The logic is simple: if importers experience an increase in income then the demand for imports would increase, and thus, trade would increase. The relationship between the compositional changes of trade and the changes in the dollar value of trade must be controlled in order to determine the amount of goods that cross the border. If trade is measured by dollar value and the composition of the trade does not change over time, then an increase in the real dollar value of trade would imply that more goods are crossing the border. However, if the composition of trade is not held constant over time, then changes in the composition of trade from low-valued goods to high-valued goods would make it appear that more goods were crossing the border than what was actually occurring. This is especially true for Mexico. Mexico was an exporter of low-valued goods, and over time they have become an exporter of high-valued goods (Economist Intelligence Unit 1992-93, 15-26). This change in composition of exports from Mexico, measured by dollar value, would exaggerate the amount of cargo crossing the border. Therefore, to determine the true level of trade between the U.S. and its contiguous neighbors, the compositional changes of trade must be controlled. The tariff rates on goods should be negatively correlated with the amount of goods traded. As tariff rates between the three countries increase, the amount of goods traded between these countries should decrease. The effect of an increase in the foreign currency exchange rate will most likely increase U.S. imports, but decrease U.S. exports. If the U.S. dollar exchanges for more foreign currency, then U.S. citizens could buy more foreign products and imports would increase. However, foreigners would not be able to buy as much U.S. produced goods, and thus, U.S. exports would decrease. To conclude, there should be a positive correlation between the foreign currency exchange rates and imports but negative for exports. There should be a positive correlation between the level of trade among the three countries and real GDP and compositional changes from low-valued to high-valued goods. However, there should be a negative correlation between the level of trade and tariff rates.

SECTION II THE DATA AND VARIABLES

5.2.1 The Data

The actual functional form of the regression model used to estimate the effects of transborder entry regulations is dictated by the availability of data. Table 5-1 presents summary statistics of variables that will be used to estimate the effects that transborder regulations have on the number of interlining service establishments along the border.

5.2.2 Interlining Service Establishments

The number of interlining service establishments located within the commercial zones around the ports of entry along the international borders will be approximated by the number of establishments within the counties containing the ports of entry. Data on the number of establishments within the counties are obtained from the *County Business Patterns*, published by Department of Commerce, under the three digit Standard Industrial Codes (SIC's) local trucking and courier services (SIC 421), warehousing and storage (SIC 422), and

Table 5-1: Table of Descriptive Statistics

Variables	U.S.-MEXICO		U.S.-CANADA	
	Mean	Std. Dev.	Mean	Std. Dev.
Local Trucking and Courier Service Establishments (SIC 421) per county	143.02	144.54	205.85	199.33
Warehousing Establishments (SIC 422) per county	22.37	27.40	17.68	20.07
Transportation Arrangement Establishments (SIC 473) per county	60.00	52.90	29.27	35.40
Inbound Trucks per port of entry	210,615	127,241.9	370,273.5	358,004
Custom District Imports ($ millions)	33.63	20.32	126.43	94.88
Dutiable Value/ Custom Value	0.6671	0.13	0.29	0.08
Percent Imports Agricultural	12.88	7.14	8.01	1.45
Percent Import Manufacturing	40.86	16.54	77.77	4.10
Real U.S. GDP (billions $)	4,196.51	457.85	4,196.51	457.85
Tariff Rate	71.05	9.09	27.01	1.92
Exchange Rate	0.99	1.19	1.22	0.08

arrangement for transportation for freight and cargo (SIC 473).[7] These SIC's capture the basic elements involved in interlining international cargo, that is, the basic elements of the transference of goods through time, space, and form. The time span of the data is from 1978 to 1991.

Generally, the counties containing the ports of entry are larger than the commercial zones that they approximate, but in some cases the counties are nearly the same size as the commercial zones. In a few cases, the counties are smaller than the commercial zones. The port of El Paso has a commercial zone that is nearly the same size as the county of El Paso, TX. The port of Detroit has a commercial zone that completely surrounds the county of Wayne, MI, and encroaches four other counties. To the extent that most of the interlining service establishments are located near the actual ports of entry, well within the county, and are sufficiently included under the SIC 421, 422 and 473, then this procedure will capture most of the interlining service establishments at the ports of entry. Attention will be focused on four main ports of entry along each border. The ports of entry are San Diego, CA; Nogales, AZ; El Paso, TX; Laredo, TX, along the U.S.-Mexican Border, and Pembina, ND; Detroit, MI; Buffalo, NY; and Ogdensburg, NY, along the U.S.-Canadian border. From 1978 to 1991, the mean per county number of local trucking and courier service establishments, SIC 421, along the U.S.-Mexican border is 143.20, along the U.S.-Canadian border the number of establishments per county is 205.85. The mean number of Warehousing and Storage establishments, SIC 422, along the U.S.-Mexican border is 22.37 per county, while along the U.S.-Canadian border the mean number is 17.68. There are 60 establishments used to arrange transportation for freight and cargo, SIC 473, per county along the U.S.-Mexican border, and along the U.S.-Canadian border the number of establishments is 29.27.

5.2.3 Trucks Crossing the Border

Data on the number of trucks crossing the ports of entry are obtained from the Department of Customs' computer and microfiche files. The U.S. Customs Service keeps records on the number of inbound trucks entering the U.S. The number of outbound trucks is not recorded.[8] Therefore, the number of inbound trucks will serve as a proxy for the variable *trucks* in the model above.

Because of the cost of collecting the data, only the number of inbound trucks from 1978 to 1993 through eight ports of entry (four for each border) was available. The selected ports of entry along the U.S.-Mexican border are San Diego, CA; Nogales, AZ; El Paso, TX, and Laredo, TX. The ports of entry along the U.S.-Canadian border are Pembina, ND; Detroit, MI; Buffalo, NY; and Ogdensburg, NY. In terms of the number of inbound trucks passing through Customs in 1993, the four ports of entry along the U.S.-Mexican border were the busiest of all the southern ports of entry, with port of Laredo as the busiest, followed by El Paso, San Diego, and Nogales. Of the four ports of entry along the U.S.-Canadian border, the port of Detroit handles the most trucks followed by the port of Buffalo. The port of Pembina ranks fourth in terms of the number of inbound truck crossings, and the port of Ogdensburg ranks nineteenth out of a total of eight-six northern ports of entry.

The counties have the same name as the ports of entry. The exceptions are the counties of Webb, TX, which contains the port of Laredo; Santa Cruz, AZ, which contains the port of Nogales; Saint Lawrence, NY, which contains the port of Ogdensburg, and the county of Erie, NY, which contains the port of Buffalo. From 1978 to 1993, at each of the four ports of entry along the U.S.-Mexican border there were an average of 210,615 inbound truck crossings, and for the U.S.-Canadian border, there were 370,273.5 inbound truck crossings.

5.2.4 International Trade

The real value of imports into the U.S. from Mexico and Canada passing through the Custom districts of San Diego, CA; Nogales, AZ; El Paso, TX, and Laredo, TX for the U.S.-Mexican border, and the Custom districts of Pembina, ND; Detroit, MI; Buffalo, NY, and Ogdensburg, NY along the U.S.-Canadian border will be used to measure the amount of trade between the three countries. This variable will be called *rportimp* (real port-level imports). The decision to use imports as a measure of the volume of trade was greatly influenced by the availability of data on truck crossings. The number of inbound trucks crossing the U.S. international borders are moste likely to be influenced by the level of imports. It is not very likely that exports from the U.S. would greatly influence the number of inbound trucks into the U.S. For this reason, exports were not included as a measure of trade. Also the time span of *rportimp* was greatly influenced by the time span of the data on truck crossings. The time span of the data for *rportimp* will be from 1977 to 1993. The data on the imports through the four Custom districts along each border were collected from the government publications, *Merchandise Trade: Selected Highlights* and *Highlights of U.S. Export and Import Trade* from the Foreign Trade Division of the Bureau of the Census (1977-88; 1989-93). At the mean value for the Custom district along each border between the years 1977-93, the U.S.-Mexican border saw $33.63 million imports, while the U.S.-Canadian border saw $126.43 million worth of imports.

5.2.5 Regulation Variables

The two borders, the U.S.-Canadian border and the U.S.-Mexican border, have undergone unique regulatory regime changes since 1980. Time-specific dummy variables will be created to estimate the impact of the regime changes on the number of establishments that locate along these borders. Two sets of dummy variables will be formed, one set for the policies that affect the U.S.-Canadian border, and one set for the policies that affect the U.S.-Mexican border.

For the U.S.-Canadian border, two dummy variables are created, one variable associated with the Motor Carrier Act of 1980 called *"mca80,"* and another variable associated with the Motor Vehicle Transportation Act of 1987 called *"mvta87."* The *mca80* variable denotes the U.S. decision to open the U.S. side of the northern border to Canadian truckers. It takes on the value of one for the years after 1979, and zero otherwise. The dummy variable *mvta87* denotes the period in time when Canada decided to open the border to U.S. truckers, and it takes on the value of one for the years after 1986, and zero otherwise.

For the U.S.-Mexican border, three dummy variables are created. One variable will be associated with the Motor Carrier Act of 1980 called *"mca80,"* one associated with the Bus Regulatory Reform Act of 1982 called *"brra82,"* and one associated with the Motor Carrier Safety Act of 1984 called *"mcsa84."* The *mca80* variable represents the period in time when the U.S. side of the border was open to Mexican truckers. This variable will take the value of one for the years of 1980 and 1981, and zero otherwise. In 1982, the President of the United States closed the border to Mexican truckers carrying ICC regulated cargo. The variable *brra82* represents this closure, and takes on the value of one for the years 1982 through 1984, and zero otherwise. The variable *mcsa84* represents the full closure of the southern border to Mexican carriers under the Motor Carrier Safety Act. This variable takes on the value of one for the years after 1983, and zero otherwise.

5.2.6 Cargo Composition

Data were collected for two variables that are proposed to control for compositional changes of cargo that trucks transport into the U.S. The compositional changes of imported goods will generally indicate institutional changes of the exporting countries which affect the value and quantity of cargo crossing the border. The two variables are the percentage of the agricultural goods exported from Mexico and Canada, *pctAG*, and the ratio of the dutiable value of imports to the total Custom value of imports entering the U.S. through each of the eight Custom districts listed above. This variable will be called *portcomp*.

A time series of the percentage of the agricultural goods exported from Canada and Mexico will show yearly aggregate changes in the composition of goods imported into the U.S. from these countries. The United States is the largest importer of both Canadian and Mexican goods. Approximately 75 percent of all Canadian exports are purchased by the United States (Mercer Management Consulting 1992, 35). For Mexico, the U.S. accounts for approximately 82 percent of all Mexican exports (Department of State 1994, 1-2). Because the U.S. is the largest importer of the goods from these two countries, the changes in the percentage of agricultural goods exported from Canada and Mexico will generally indicate the compositional changes of their imports to the U.S. Thus, holding the dollar value of imports constant, if *pctAG* increases, we would expect to see more trucks in total crossing the border. The reason is that agricultural goods generally have lower value to weight or volume than manufactured goods. Thus, for a given dollar value of imports, it would take more agricultural goods to equal the same dollar value of manufactured goods. Therefore, more truckers would be needed to transport the agricultural goods. Whether the compositional change is through reductions in import tariffs or though some other national promotional program makes little difference. The variable *pctAG* is used to control for the national-level shifts in composition of cargo and to avoid specification bias that may affect the estimates of the effects of entry regulations in the upcoming regression model. However, the *pctAG* captures only the effects that national-level compositional changes in trade would have on the total number of truck crossings. It does not control for the changes at each individual port of entry.

Though the aggregate composition of imports may appear stable over time, there may be tremendous changes occurring across each Custom district. It is these sector changes that makes *portcomp* a desirable statistic to include in the analysis. The variable *portcomp* is the ratio of the dutiable value of imports to the total Custom value of imports entering the U.S. at each of the four Custom districts along each border. It should be noted that the dutiable value of imports is *not* the amount of duties collected on the imported goods. It represents, in general, the percentage of the value of the goods subject to duties. The *Harmonized Tariff Schedule of the United States* (U.S. International Trade Commission, 1995) lists dutiable rates on goods imported into the United States based on a percentage of the quantity and/or quality of the imported goods. The assigned rates are applied to all goods imported into the U.S. regardless of the country of exportation. Specific exceptions to the dutiable rates are annotated in the schedule. These exceptions apply to specific countries entering into trade agreements with the U.S. However, the general dutiable rates assigned to the particular goods listed in the schedule do not change. Therefore, the actual duties collected from the goods in the trade agreement with the U.S. would be less than the listed dutiable values indicated in the tariff schedule. For example, the unweighted mean dutiable rates on manufactured goods is roughly 6.86 percent of the value of the imported good and the dutiable rates on agriculture goods is 8.47 percent.[9] Through trade agreements with Mexico (prior to 1965), manufactured goods produced in the Maquiladora industries are imported into the U.S. duty free (some goods have a value added tariff). This means the actual amount of duties collected on Maquiladora manufactured goods is zero, but the dutiable value of goods listed in the Tariff Schedule would be approximately 6.86 percent of the value of the goods.

A typical scenario when the general dutiable rates change in the tariff schedule is through trade negotiations affecting several countries. For example, General Agreement on Trade and Tariffs (GATT) would require changes in the dutiable rates on nearly all imported goods. In this case, the entire tariff schedule will be changed to comply with the lower tariff rates agreed on by the GATT members. In general, these GATT agreements affect tariff rates slowly over time. Also, the U.S. protects agricultural goods more than most other imports, and even with GATT agreements, agricultural goods will generally have higher dutiable rates (Warf and Cox 1993, 348-9). For any given year, tariff rates across Custom districts are constant, and tariff rates in general are slow moving over time, any variation in the ratio of dutiable value to total value will be due to changes in composition of imports.

The variable *portcomp* controls for the changes in the composition of cargo at each Custom district. Based on the nature of the dutiable rates, agricultural imports typically have higher dutiable rates than manufacturing imports. This implies that yearly increases in *portcomp* for a particular Custom district will indicate a compositional change toward more agricultural intensive imports passing though that Custom district. Thus, holding all other variables constant, increases in *portcomp* for a typical Custom district should be positively correlated with the number of inbound trucks crossing that Custom district.[10] This Custom district level argument is the same as the argument proposed for *pctAG* at the aggregate level. That is, holding the value of imports constant, an increase in the proportion of agricultural imports that pass through a Custom district would require more trucks to haul the cargo. The reason is that agricultural goods have lower dollar value than manufactured goods; thus, it takes more agricultural cargo to equal the same dollar value of manufactured goods. Thus, more trucks would be needed to haul the extra cargo. Therefore, like *pctAG* at the aggregate level, *portcomp* detects compositional changes at the Custom district level and should be positively correlated with the number of inbound truck crossings.

The data collected on *pctAG* come from the United Nations, *The International Trade Statistics Yearbook*. The data collected on *portcomp* come from government publications: *Merchandise Trade: Selected Highlights*, and *Highlights of U.S. Export and Import Trade*, from the Foreign Trade Division of the Bureau of the Census (1977-88; 1989-93). The time span of the data is from 1977 to 1992 for *pctAG*,[11] and from 1977 to 1993 for *portcomp*. From Table 5-1, the mean values of *portcomp* (Dutiable Value/ Custom Value) is 0.6671 for imports across the U.S.-Mexican border and 0.08 across the U.S.-Canadian border. From 1977 to 1993, the percentage of agricultural imports from Mexico is 12.88 and from Canada the percentage is 8.01.

5.2.7 Real Gross Domestic Product

The variable *rGDP* is used in the regression model to capture shifts in the demand for U.S. imports due to changes in U.S. aggregate incomes. Data for *rGDP* is obtained from the *Economic Report of the President* (Council of Economic Advisers 1994). The data spans the years 1977 to 1993. Because the analysis is focusing on imports into the U.S., the real GDP from Canada and Mexico would not likely influence U.S. imports; therefore, these statistics were excluded from the model.

5.2.8 Tariff Rate

The tariff rates placed on imports entering the U.S. will be proxied by taking the ratio of the sum of the dutiable value of imports to the sum of the total Custom value of imports for the four Custom districts along each border. This variable will be called *tariff*. The variable controls for changes in the dutiable rates on imports that occur when there are major changes in the tariff schedule of the U.S. Though these changes occur slowly, they would have the biggest effect on imports. The changes in the tariff rates would cause the ratio of the aggregated dutiable value to total value of imports to change in a like manner. Therefore, in a regression of the real dollar value of imports on the variable *tariff*, it is expected that the sign of the coefficient on this variable will be negative. However, one could argue that the aggregation of the ratio of dutiable to the total Custom value of imports, along with the influence of tariff changes, would be picking up changes caused by nationwide shifts in the composition of traded goods. If this were the case, we would also expect a negative coefficient on this variable as well. For example, Mexico has moved from exporting agricultural goods to exporting manufactured goods nationwide. Therefore, the shift in the compositional change is from low-valued, high-tariff agricultural goods to high-valued, low-tariff manufactured goods. In this case, a decrease in *tariff* would indicate an overall increase in manufactured imports entering the U.S. Thus, the negative relationship between imports, measured by value, and the *tariff* variable would occur.

There is evidence to suggest that *tariff* does not detect nationwide composition changes. The simple correlation coefficients between *tariff* and *pctAG* from U.S.-Canada, and U.S.-Mexico, over the years 1978 to 1992, are -0.1855 and 0.0845, respectively. There is little correlation (and also mixed signs) between the aggregate compositional changes indicated by the percent of agriculture goods exported, *pctAG*, and *tariff*. This suggests that *tariff* is not picking up nationwide compositional changes. Thus, the variation in *tariff* would most likely be due to the changes in the tariff rates on imported goods.

5.2.9 The Foreign Currency Exchange Rate

The foreign currency exchange rate, *exchgrte*, is used to capture the effects that variations in the exchange rates may have on the imports coming into the U.S. The data for the variable *exchgrte* are obtained from *International Financial Statistics Yearbook* (International Monetary Fund 1994, 516-7). This statistic is the ratio of the foreign currency to the U.S. dollar.[12] Since trade is measured in terms of imports, there should be a positive correlation between *exchgrte* and the variable *rportimp*. All data are annual, and the time span is from 1977 to 1992.

SECTION III: ECONOMETRIC MODEL AND RESULTS

5.3.1 The Econometric Model

Three regression equations were formed corresponding to the basic theoretical model from section 5.1.4. After experimenting with functional forms, the following regressions were judged to be the best.

$Estab^j_{i,t}$ $= \alpha_0 + \alpha_1 \, truck_{i,t} + REG \, \alpha_2 + port \, \alpha_3 + \varepsilon_{i,t}$ (5.1)

$\ln(truck_{i,t})$ $= \beta_0 + \beta_1 \, rportimp_{i,t} + \beta_2 \, pctAG_t + \beta_3 \, portcomp_{i,t} + REG$
$\beta_4 + port \, \beta_5 + \mu_{i,t}$ (5.2)

$rportimp_{i,t}$ $= \phi_0 + f_1 \, rGDP_t + \phi_2 \, pctAG_t + \phi_3 tariff_t + \phi_4 \, exchgate_t +$
$port \, \phi_5 + n_{i,t}$ (5.3)

$j \in$ {SIC 421, SIC 422, SIC 473}

$i \in$ Detroit, Buffalo, Pembina, Ogdensburg for the U.S.-Canadian border.
San Diego, Nogales, Laredo, El Paso for the U.S.-Mexican border.

$Estab^j_{i,t}$ = the number of j establishments around port i at time t. $1977 \leq t \leq 1991$.

$truck_{i,t}$ = the number of inbound trucks at port i during time t. $1978 \leq t \leq 1993$.[13]

$rportimp_{i,t}$ = the real Custom value of U.S. imports through port of entry i along either the U.S.- Mexican border or the U.S.-Canada border at time t. $1977 \leq t \leq 1992$.

$portcomp_{i,t}$ = the ratio of the dutiable value to total Custom value of imports at each port of entry i at time t. $1977 \leq t \leq 1993$.

$rGDP_t$ = the United States real gross domestic product at time t. $1977 \leq t \leq 1993$.

$tariff_t$ = the ratio of the cumulative dutiable value to the cumulative total Customs value of imports through the four ports of entry along either U.S.-Mexican or U.S.-Canadian border at time t. $1977 \leq t \leq 1993$.

$exchgrate_t$ = the ratio of the foreign currency to U.S. currency at time t. $1977 \leq t \leq 1993$.

REG   = a vector of:

               *mca*80, *brra*82, and *mcsa*84 for the U.S.-Mexican border.

               *mca*80, and *mvta*87 for the U.S.-Canadian border.

port   = a vector of dummy variables taking on the value of 1 for each port of entry in the model, and zero otherwise.

$pctAG_t$ = the percent of Mexican or Canadian agricultural exports. $1977 \leq t \leq 1993$.

The regressions were run using the data from the U.S.-Canadian border, then applying the same functional form, the regressions were run with data corresponding to the U.S.-Mexican border.

The parameters for equation (5.3) were estimated by regressing *rportimp* on *pctAG*, *rGDP*, *tariff*, *exchgrte*, and *port*. For the Custom districts that showed evidence of serial correlation, the Cochrane-Orcutt procedure was performed to correct this problem. If the Durbin-Watson statistic was less than d_U (the upper bound of the statistic), then the Cochrane-Orcutt procedure was performed on that district's data.[14] There was evidence of heteroskedasticity across each Custom district. To correct for heteroskedasticity a Huber's correction procedure (also known as White's correction) was used.[15]

Equation (5.2) was estimated by regressing the natural log of the number of inbound trucks, *truck*, on the instrumental variable for *rportimp*, the variables *portcomp*, *REG,* and *port* by a two stage least squares (2SLS) method. The 2SLS method was used because *rportimp* is endogenous to the system. For the ports of entry that showed evidence of serial correlation the Cochrane-Orcutt procedure was performed on the data for that port sector. If the Durbin-Watson statistic was less than d_U (the upper bound of the statistic), then the Cochrane-Orcutt procedure was performed on that sector's data. To correct for heteroskedasticity Huber's or White's correction was used. There was no evidence of cross-sectional correlation (contemporaneous correlation of observations between the ports of entry), and thus, no correction was needed.

Equation (5.1) was estimated by regressing *Estab* on the instrumental variable for *truck*, the vector *REG*, and *port* using a 2SLS method. The 2SLS method was used here because *truck* is an endogenous variable in equation (5.1). For the ports of entry that showed evidence of serial correlation the Cochrane-Orcutt procedure was performed within that port sector's data. If the Durbin-Watson statistic was less than d_U, then the Cochrane-Orcutt procedure was performed on that sector's data. There was also evidence of heteroskedasticity across ports of entry. To correct for heteroskedasticity a Huber's or White's correction to the data was used. There was no evidence of cross-sectional correlation, and thus, no correction was needed.

5.3.2 The Regression Results

The results of the above regressions are shown in Tables 5-3 and 5-4. Table 5-3 lists the estimated parameters from the regression equations (5.2) and (5.3) for both borders. Table 5-4 displays the parameter estimates for regression equation (5.1) for each of the three-digit SIC establishments for each border.

5.3.2.1 Equations (5.3): Real Imports

The U.S.-Canada Border

The first column of Table 5-3 under the heading "U.S.-Canadian Border: rportimp" lists the estimated parameters for the regression describing the real value of U.S. imports from Canada (5.3). The coefficient on the variable *pctAG* is negative, as expected, and is significantly less than zero at a 5 percent level. Holding all other factors constant, a one percentage point increase in agricultural goods exported from Canada should decrease the real dollar value of U.S. imports by $6.74 million per Custom district on average. The coefficient on *rGDP* is positive, as expected, and is significantly greater than zero at a 1 percent level. For a $1 billion increase in the U.S. real Gross Domestic Product it is estimated that on average imports through each Custom district along the U.S.-Canadian border increase by $42.6 thousand. The coefficient on the variable *tariff* has the expected sign, negative, but it is not significantly different from zero. The foreign currency exchange rate is positive, which is the expected sign, but it too is not significantly different from zero.

The U.S.-Mexican Border

The third column of Table 5-3 under the heading "U.S.-Mexican Border: *rportimp*" lists the estimated parameters of the regression describing the real value of U.S. imports from Mexico. The results from regression (5.3) show the coefficient on *pctAG* is positive, which is the reverse of what was expected. Though the sign on this variable is positive, its magnitude is small (practically zero), and it is not significantly different from zero. The coefficient on the variable *rGDP*, the real Gross Domestic Product of the U.S., is positive as expected, and is significantly greater than zero at a 1 percent level. If real GDP of the U.S. increases by $1 billion, then we estimate that on average the real value of U.S. imports will increase by $15.1 thousand per Custom district. The coefficient on the variable *tariff* has the expected negative sign but it is not significantly different from zero. The coefficient on the variable *exchgrte* is positive and significantly greater than zero at a 1 percent level. With a one percent increase in the foreign currency exchange rate between the Mexican Peso and the U.S. dollar we would expect an increase in Mexican imports by $5.22 million per Custom district.

5.3.2.2 Equation (5.2): Inbound Trucks at the Borders

The U.S.-Canadian Border

In Table 5-3, the column labeled "U.S.-Canadian Border: ln(*truck*)" lists the parameter estimates from regression (5.2) associated with the logged value of the number of inbound trucks through the four ports of entry along the U.S.-Canadian border.[16] The coefficient on *rportimp*, has the expected sign, positive, and is significantly greater than zero at a 1 percent level. If imports increase by $1 million per Custom district, then it is estimated that on average the number of inbound trucks will increase by 2.7 percent per port of entry along the U.S.-Canadian border. The coefficient on the variable *portcomp*, representing the composition of cargo crossing each Custom district, has the expected sign and is significantly greater than zero at a 1 percent level. Holding all other variables constant, if *portcomp* increases by one unit (meaning, the composition of imports passing through each Custom district changes from manufactured goods to more agricultural goods by one percentage point), then we would expect on average the number of inbound trucks to increase by 9.0 percent per port of entry. That is, holding the value of imports constant, it takes 9 percent more trucks to transport low-valued cargo than it takes to transport the same dollar value of high-valued cargo. Similarly, the sign of the coefficient on the variable *pctAG* is significantly greater than zero at a 1 percent level. If the aggregate level of imports from Canada changes from manufactured goods to agricultural goods by one percentage point, we estimate that on average we will find a 28.13 percent increase in the number of inbound trucks passing though each port of entry. The coefficient on the variable *mca80*, representing the Motor Carrier Act (MCA) of 1980 which deregulated the U.S. side of the U.S.-Canadian border, is positive as expected, but it is not significantly different from zero. The MCA appears not to have significantly increased the number of inbound trucks crossing the U.S.-Canadian border. The reason for this result could be due to the fact that prior to MCA, Canadian truckers could enter the U.S. but could only operate within the commercial zones around the ports of entry. Thus, by allowing Canadian truckers to single-line shipments, the number of truck crossings would not necessarily change, only the number interlinings would change. The coefficient on the variable, *mvta87*, representing the Motor Vehicle Transportation Act (MVTA) that deregulated the Canadian side of the border, is negative and significantly less than zero at a 1 percent level. The magnitude of this effect is surprisingly strong. The MVTA reduced the number of inbound trucks into the U.S. by 31.29 percent per port of entry. The reduction in inbound trucks through the ports of Buffalo, Detroit, Ogdensburg, and Pembina suggest that entry shifted to other ports after MVTA was past. One possible reason for this result is that the ports of Buffalo, Detroit, Ogdensburg, and Pembina, being some of the busiest of the 86 ports of entry along the U.S.-Canadian border, were better suited for interlining cargo. After MVTA and interlining was not mandatory, any port along the border was suitable for entry. Inbound trucks were no longer tied to the ports of Buffalo, Detroit, Ogdensburg, and Pembina, thus the number of inbound trucks decreased, and picked up at the other ports. Verification of this supposition will be reserved for future research.

The U.S.-Mexican Border

The last column in Table 5-3, labeled "U.S.-Mexican Border: ln(*truck*)," lists the parameter estimates from regression (5.2) using the data corresponding to the U.S.-Mexican border. The variable *rportimp*, the real Custom value of imports for each port of entry, is positive as expected and is significantly greater than zero at a 1 percent level. If the real Custom value of imports through each port of entry increases by $1 million, it is expected that the number of inbound trucks will increase by 1.56 percent per port of entry. The variable *portcomp*, representing the compositional change of imports at the port level, has the expected positive sign, but is not significantly different from zero. The variable *pctAG*, representing the compositional change in the aggregate level of imports from Mexico, is positive and significantly greater than zero at a 5 percent level. This means that a one point increase in the percentage of agricultural goods exported from Mexico will on average increase the number of inbound trucks by 0.62 percent per port of entry. This is because, holding the value of cargo constant, it takes more low-valued agricultural goods to equal the same dollar value of high-valued manufactured goods. Thus, more trucks would be needed to transport the extra cargo. The coefficient on *mca80* representing the Motor Carrier Act (MCA) of 1980 is positive, however, the coefficient on this variable is not significantly different from zero. Thus, it appears that MCA did not significantly increase the number of inbound truck crossings from Mexico. However, this could be due to the fact that Mexican truckers could enter the U.S. prior to MCA but only operate within the commercial zones around the ports of entry. Thus once single-lining was possible for Mexican truckers the number of interlinings decreased, and the number of truck crossings may have increased but not significantly. Both of the coefficients on the variables *brra82* and *mcsa84*, the Bus Regulatory Reform Act (BRRA) and the Motor Carrier Safety Act (MCSA), respectively, appear to have had a significant negative effect on the number of inbound truckers crossing the southern border. The regression results show that the BRRA on average reduced the number of inbound trucks into the U.S. by 32.8 percent per port of entry. The MCSA of 1984, which was implemented two years after BRRA, reduced the number of inbound trucks into the U.S. by 32.3 percent per port of entry.

5.3.2.3 Equation (5.1): Trucking Establishments

The U.S.-Canadian Border

Under the section "421 - Local Trucking and Courier Service: U.S.-Can." in Table 5-4, the estimate of the coefficient on the variable *truck* is positive as expected and is significantly greater than zero at the 10 percent level. An increase of 100,000 inbound trucks through a port of entry would increase the demand for interlining services enough to support 5.1 new local trucking and courier service establishments at that port of entry. The variable *mca80*, representing the Motor Carrier Act (MCA) of 1980, shows that MCA had a decreasing effect on the number of establishments along the border. At a significance level of 1 percent, the MCA reduced the demand for local trucking and courier services such that an average of 17.2 establishments left each port of entry along the U.S.-Canadian border. The variable *mvta87*, which represents the Motor Vehicle Transportation Act (MVTA) of 1987 that opened the Canadian side of the U.S.-Canadian border to U.S. truckers, is positive and significantly greater than zero at a 1 percent level. The MVTA increased the demand for local trucking and courier services at the border such that 27.6 new establishments were supported at each port of entry. As discussed earlier, this suggests that the rules against cabotage became binding and the demand for services at the border to fill empty backhauls increased by a greater degree than the reduction in the demand of interlining services. Thus, deregulation of entry into Canada, after the U.S. side of the border was already deregulated, increased the demand for services to fill empty backhauls such that it could support an increase of 27.6 new local trucking and courier service establishments at each port of entry.

The section of Table 5-4 labeled "422 - Public Warehousing and Storage: U.S.-Can." shows that the variable representing inbound trucks, *truck*, is positive, but it is not significantly different from zero. This suggests that inbound trucks did not significantly affect the number of warehousing and storage establishments that locate around the ports of entry. Thus, warehousing and storage establishments may not be an appropriate measure to proxy interlining services. This is confirmed by Lasky (1995): warehouses are not an integral part of the supply chain for transborder shipping but are used as storage places to hold cargo as collateral for bank loans (also see Farver 1993, 6). This is further evidenced by the coefficients on the variables *mca80* and *mvta87* not being significantly different from zero.

The section of Table 5-4 labeled "473 - Arrangement for Transport for Freight: U.S.-Can." shows that the coefficient on the number of inbound trucks, *truck*, is positive and significantly greater than zero at the 1 percent level. This result suggests that an increase of 100,000 trucks through each port of entry on average would increase the demand for interlining services such that it could support an increase of 5.7 new establishments involved in the arrangement for transportation of freight and cargo at each port of entry. The coefficient on the variable *mca80*, representing the Motor Carrier Act (MCA) of 1980 which opened the U.S. side of the U.S.-Canadian border, is negative as predicted and significantly less than zero at the 5 percent level. The MCA appears to have decreased the demand for services for the arrangement for transportation for freight and cargo by 2.9 establishments per port of entry. The variable *mvta87*, representing the Motor Vehicle Transportation Act (MVTA), is positive and significantly greater than zero at the 1 percent level. Again this suggests, given that the U.S. side of the border was already deregulated, the deregulation of the Canadian side of the border made rules against cabotage a constraining factor. The MVTA increased the demand for services to fill empty backhauls such that the number of establishments involved in the arrangement for transportation for freight and cargo increased by 7.0 establishments per port of entry.

The U.S.-Mexican Border

The section of the Table 5-4 labeled "421 - Local Trucking and Courier Service: U.S.-Mex." shows the variable *truck* is positive, as expected, and is significantly greater than zero at the 1 percent level. It is estimated that if the number of inbound trucks increase by 100,000 through each port of entry, then the demand for interlining services will increase enough to support 28.3 new local trucking and courier service establishments per port of entry. The variable *mca80*, which represents the Motor Carrier Act (MCA) that opened the U.S. side of the U.S.-Mexican border, is negative, as expected, and significantly less than zero at the 1 percent level. It appears that the MCA reduced the demand for interlining services such that local trucking and courier service establishments decreased by 46.4 establishments per port of entry. The variable *brra82*, representing the Bus Regulatory Reform Act (BRRA) which partially closed the U.S. side of the U.S.-Mexican border, is positive as expected and is significantly greater than zero at the 5 percent level. It appears that since BRRA restricted Mexican truckers from entering the U.S., the demand for local trucking and courier services increased such that 16.4 new establishments were supported at each port of entry. The variable *mcsa84*, representing the Motor Carrier Safety Act which was a stronger barrier to entry for Mexican truckers than BRRA, increased the demand for local trucking and courier services such that 34.9 new establishments were supported at each port of entry.

The section of Table 5-4 labeled "422 - Public Warehousing and Storage: U.S.-Mex." shows that the number of inbound trucks, *truck*, significantly increased the number of establishments that located along the U.S.-Mexican border. With an increase of 100,000 trucks through each port of entry we would expect to see an increase of 5.3 establishments involved in warehousing and storage. However, there is evidence again suggesting that warehousing and storage establishments may not be an appropriate proxy for interlining service establishments. The reason for this is because of the conflicting results from MCA and BRRA. The coefficient on the variable *mca80* is positive, which is not as expected, but it is not significantly different from zero. The coefficient on the variable *brra82*, though significantly different from zero, is negative, which is theoretically the wrong sign. Given that the number of inbound trucks increased the demand for warehousing and storage establishments, the insignificance and theoretically wrong signs on the policy parameters suggest that warehousing and storage establishments are not good proxies for the establishments involved in interlining transborder trucks.

The section of Table 5-4 labeled "473- Arrangement for Transportation for Freight: U.S.-Mex." shows that the number of inbound trucks, *truck*, significantly increased the number of establishments involved in the arrangement for transportation of freight and cargo. An increase of 100,000 inbound trucks through each port of entry increased the demand for interlining services such that it supported 5.3 new establishments involved in the arrangement for transportation for freight and cargo at each port of entry. The variables *mca80* and *brra82* have the expected sign, but they are not significantly different from zero. The variable *mcsa84*, representing a period in time of increased entry regulation, is positive and significantly greater than zero at the 1 percent level. During this period, the Motor Carrier Safety Act caused the demand for interlining services to increase such that 8.0 more establishments per port of entry could be supported.

5.3.2.4 Comparing Mexico's and Canada's Results

Comparing the results of the regressions for the U.S.-Canadian border to the results for the U.S.-Mexican border illustrates the dichotomy of transborder trucking. From Table 5-3, under the headings "U.S.-Canadian Border: *rportimp*" and "U.S.-Mexican: *rportimp*," Canadian imports into the U.S. should increase by $42.6 thousand for each $1 billion increase in the U.S. real GDP, while Mexican imports should increase by $15.1 thousand. The difference in the results comes about because the Canadian economy is more integrated with the U.S. than the Mexican economy. The U.S. has traditionally had good trade relations with Canada, but it has been only fairly recent that trade relations between the U.S. and Mexico have become more open. Thus, over time, small changes in the real GDP of the U.S. economy would affect Canadian exports more than Mexican exports. Also, looking at the foreign currency exchange rate, Mexico's exchange rate has a significant effect on exports from Mexico, while the Canadian exchange rate shows no significant effect. This result is due to the variances in the two countries' exchange rates over time. The Canadian foreign currency exchange rate has been relatively stable over the years compared to the Mexican foreign currency exchange rate. The larger variation in the Mexican exchange rate would cause detectable changes in the balance of trade. The smaller variation in the Canadian exchange rate would most likely not cause detectable effects on trade.

Looking at the regressions under the heading "U.S.-Canadian Border: ln(*truck*)" and "U.S.-Mexican Border: ln(*truck*)," the regressions show that with an equal increase in the real dollar-value of imports, the number of inbound trucks from Canada would increase by a greater percentage than the number of inbound trucks from Mexico. A possible reason for this result is due to the difference in the types of goods carried by the two nations' trucks. Canadian inbound truckloads may carry a higher percentage of low-valued goods, while Mexican truckloads may have a higher percentage of high-valued goods. An equal increase in the dollar value of imports into the U.S. would increase Canadian truck crossings more than it would increase Mexican truck crossings. To get an idea of cargo carried by inbound trucks, Table 5-5 lists estimates of the percentage and type of cargo carried by truck into the U.S. from Mexico. Similar statistics are not available for Canada. Without comparable statistics from Canada, the notion that Canadian truckloads have lower value than Mexican truckloads is purely conjecture.

Looking at Table 5-4, comparing the effects that an increase in the number of inbound trucks have on the number of establishments that locate at a port of entry, the U.S.-Canadian border shows that an increase of 100,000 inbound trucks would increase the number of local trucking and courier service establishments (SIC 421) by 5.2 establishments, while the U.S.-Mexican border would experience an increase of 28.3 establishments. Measuring the percentage change in the number of SIC 421 establishments caused by the percentage change in the number of inbound trucks, the U.S.-Canadian border has an elasticity of 0.10, while the U.S.-Mexican border has an elasticity of 0.45. The U.S.-Mexican border appears to be more sensitive to a change in the number inbound trucks than the U.S.-Canadian border. This result is reversed for establishments involved in the arrangement for transportation for freight and cargo (SIC 473) where the elasticity for these establishments along the U.S.-Mexican border is 0.18, while the elasticity for the U.S.-Canadian border is 0.61. This reversal of elasticities could be a result of the superior trucking network developed between the U.S. and Canada.[17] Well-developed networks do not exist between the U.S. and Mexico. By networking in a hub-and-spoke fashion, trucking firms can internalize the services offered by private transportation brokers, but hub-and-spoke networking requires extensive use of local trucking. Thus, when the number of inbound trucks increased along the U.S.-Canadian border we would expect to find a greater need for local trucking and courier services rather than the services to arrange for transportation for freight and cargo. This would be the reverse for the U.S.-Mexican border. Mexico has not developed the hub-and-spoke networking used extensively by the LTL industry (Gooley 1991, 48). Thus, Mexican truckers must rely on private brokerage services to arrange for the transportation of their freight once in the U.S. Because Mexico does not have well-developed hub-and-spoke networks in the U.S., as the number of inbound trucks crossing the U.S.-Mexican border increases, we would expect to see an increased demand for services to arrange for the transportation of freight and cargo. This demand would naturally be greater than the demand for local trucking and courier services.

Looking at the effects of the U.S. Motor Carrier Act shows that once the U.S. side of the borders were opened to foreign truckers, the U.S.-Canadian border lost 17.2 local trucking and courier service establishments while the U.S.-Mexican border lost 46.4 establishments per port of entry. In terms of percentage change in 1991, the U.S.-Canadian border experienced roughly a 2 percent decrease in the number of establishments per port of entry compared to a 5 percent decrease for the U.S.-Mexican border. The disparity between the percentages caused by the same regulatory regimes indicates the dichotomy in the nature of transborder trucking across the two borders. One reason why this dichotomy exists could come from the differences in the culture and language between the U.S. and Mexico that cannot be measured empirically. The culture and language between the U.S. and Canada is quite similar. Because of the differences between the U.S. and Mexico, the U.S.-Mexican border would require more establishments to overcome the asymmetry in information. A more likely reason for the dichotomy is because of the political relationships that existed between the U.S., Mexico, and Canada. Traditionally, U.S. trade relations with Canada concerning truck entry have been relatively relaxed compared to the trade relations that existed between the U.S. and Mexico. Though Canada maintained entry barriers similar to the U.S. prior to the MCA, Canada did allowed limited U.S. truck entry.[18] It is likely that the U.S. reciprocated this policy and allowed a greater number of single-line shipments from Canada. Mexico, on the other hand, restricted practically all U.S. carriers from crossing the border into Mexico.[19] It is likely that because Mexico denied nearly all U.S. trucks from crossing the border, the U.S. authorities were more critical in authorizing entry into the U.S. by Mexican truckers prior to MCA. This would force a greater number of interlinings along the U.S.-Mexican border compared to the U.S.-Canadian border. Thus, the marginal effect of deregulating the U.S. side of the borders would have a greater impact on the number of single-linings from Mexico and hence a greater marginal impact on the number of local trucking and courier service establishments along the U.S.-Mexican border.

5.3.3 Measuring the Effects of Regulations

The effects of transborder trucking regulations will be measured by using the parameter estimates of the variables in the vector REG from regression (5.1). These parameter estimates represent the change in the equilibrium number of establishments along the two borders caused by changes in transborder trucking policy regimes. As discussed previously, by multiplying an appropriate market price of interlining services to the change in the equilibrium number of establishments along each border, the dollar value of the effects of the regulations can be estimated.

The equilibrium market price for interlining services will be estimated by using two different measures. One measure will provide a lower bound, and the other measure will provide an upper bound on the market price for interlining services. The lower bound for the market price of interlining services will be estimated by using the average of the 1991 total annual payroll per establishment (adjusted to 1987 dollars) for the four ports of entry along each border. Thus, the lower bound represents the labor cost associated with the allocation of resources toward the border resulting from the regulations. The data for the total annual payroll per establishment is obtained from the publication *County Business Patterns* (Department of Commerce 1991). The upper bound on the market price for interlining services will be estimated by the average of the 1992 annual revenue per SIC establishment for the metropolitan areas that most closely match the ports of entry along each of the two borders. The upper bound is an estimate of the dollar value of the resources allocated toward the borders due to the regulations. The metropolitan areas used in the estimation of the upper bound on the market price for the U.S.-Mexican border are El Paso, TX; Laredo, TX; San Diego, CA, and Tuson, AZ. The metropolitan areas used to estimate the upper bound on the market price of interlining services for the U.S.-Canadian border are Detroit, MI, and Erie, NY.[20] The data for the 1992 annual revenue per establishment is obtained from the 1992 *Census of Transportation, Communications, and Utilities: Geographic Area Series: Summary*, published by the Bureau of the Census.

Multiplying the market prices for interlining services to the parameter estimates of the variables in REG from equation (5.1) will produce the measures of the effect of the entry regulations. Table 5-8 presents the parameter estimates from the regressions of equation (5.1) and the estimated dollar value of the effects of each transborder regulation. Because it was concluded that warehousing and storage did not serve as a good proxy for interlining services, the estimates are not included in the following table.

Table 5-8: Effects of Policy Changes on Transborder Trucking Establishments

| Policy Regimes | Change in the Equilibrium Number of Establishments for each SIC | | Estimated Cost of Transborder Regulations ($1000) | | | |
| | | | Lower Bound (labor cost) | | Upper Bound (total cost) | |
	421	473	421	473	421	473
BRRA	16.39	0	3,201	0	17,634	0
MCSA	34.95	8.09	6,827	1,407	37,605	17,801
MCA (U.S.-Mexico)	-46.41	0	-9,066	0	-49,934	0
MCA (U.S.-Canada)	-17.20	-2.95	-9,816	-1,184	-35,621	-2,650
MVTA	27.59	7.01	15,746	2,815	57,154	6,297

It is interesting to note that the policies that represent the closure of the U.S. side of the U.S.-Mexican border, the Bus Regulatory Reform Act (BRRA) and the Motor Carrier Safety Act (MCSA), show that more firms located along the border during these periods. This implies that resources were being diverted toward the ports of entry upon the closure of the border. The policies that opened the U.S. side of the borders, the Motor Carrier Act (MCA), shows resources were being diverted away from the borders during this period in time. The policies MCA, BRRA, and MCSA opened or closed only one side of the borders. That is, the foreign side of the two borders was closed to U.S. truckers during these policy changes. The policy that represents the opening of the Canadian side of the U.S.-Canadian border, the Motor Vehicle Transportation Act (MVTA), occurred when the U.S. side of the border was already opened. The MVTA caused resources to be diverted toward the border. The most likely reason for this phenomenon is because once single-line transborder trucking was allowed by both nations, the anti-cabotage laws of each country become binding. The anti-cabotage laws, upheld by both the U.S. and Canada, increased the likelihood of empty backhauls for the transborder truckers once inside the other country's international boundaries. The combination of the distance from the border and the probability of empty backhauls due to the anti-cabotage laws increases the expected cost of transporting international cargo. Establishments located along the border can decrease the cost of transborder trucking by consolidating freight to fill the empty trailers for homeward bound truckers. Thus, the resources allocated toward the border are not due to an increase in the number of establishments interlining cargo, but due to the increase in the number of establishments that help fill empty backhauls.

The upper and lower bounds (the total cost and labor cost, respectively) of the effects of regulations are listed under the columns labeled "Upper Bound," and "Lower Bound" in Table 5-8. For the establishments involved in local trucking and courier services, SIC 421, the Bus Regulatory Reform Act, a policy that restricted Mexican truckers from entering the U.S., caused 16.4 new establishments to located around each port of entry. This represents a resources allocation ranging from a lower bound of $3.20 million to an upper bound of $17.63 million per port of entry.

The Motor Carrier Safety Act, which restricted Mexican truckers from entering the U.S., shows on average 35.0 new local trucking and courier service establishments, SIC 421, located along each port of entry along the U.S.-Mexican border. This represents a lower bound of $6.83 million and an upper bound of $37.60 million worth of resources allocated toward each port of entry.

The Motor Carrier Act that opened the U.S. side of the U.S.-Mexican border shows that on average 46.4 local trucking and courier service establishments left each port of entry. This represents an allocation of resources with a lower bound of $9.07 million and an upper bound of $49.93 million.

The Motor Carrier Act caused 17.2 establishments to leave each port of entry along the U.S.-Canadian border. This represents a resource allocation with a lower bound of $9.82 million and an upper bound of $35.62 million per port of entry.

The Motor Vehicle Transportation Act, which opened the Canadian side of the border to U.S. truckers, shows an average of 27.6 local trucking and courier service establishments located around each port of entry. This represents a resource allocation with a lower bound of $15.75 million and an upper bound of $57.15 million per port of entry along the U.S.-Canadian border.

Under the column for SIC 473, the establishments involved in the arrangement of freight and cargo, the Motor Carrier Safety Act increased the demand for interlining services to the point that 8.1 establishments located around each port of entry. This represents a lower bound of $1.41 million and an upper bound of $17.80 million of resources allocated toward each per port of entry.

The Motor Carrier Act which opened the U.S. side of the U.S.-Canadian border decreased the demand for interlining services such that 3.0 establishments per port of entry left the border. This represents a lower bound of $1.18 million and an upper bound of $2.65 million that left each port of entry.

The Motor Vehicle Transportation Act that opened the Canadian side of the U.S.-Canadian border increased the demand for services for the arrangement for transportation of freight and cargo by 7.01 establishments per port of entry. This represents a lower bound of $2.82 million and an upper bound of $6.30 million of the resources allocated toward each port of entry along the border.

5.3.4 Conclusion

Regulations involving foreign truck entry have distorting effects. Not only do the regulations directly affect the number of trucks entering the U.S., they also affect the infrastructure along the border. Third party transportation agents locate near the ports of entry to assist in the transborder movement of goods. Estimating the change in the number of establishments used for interlining cargo along the U.S.-Mexican and U.S.-Canadian borders provide a means of measuring the distortions created by the regulations. It has been discovered that regulations that closed the U.S.-Mexican border to Mexican trucks, in particular the Bus Regulatory Reform Act of 1982 and the Motor Carrier Safety Act of 1984, caused $55 million worth of resources in the form of interlining service establishments ($3.2 million represents labor resources) to locate at each port of entry on average. The opening of the U.S. side of the U.S.-Mexican and U.S.-Canadian border by the Motor Carrier Act of 1980 caused establishments that provide interlining services to move away from the two borders. It is estimated that the exodus of establishments is a per port of entry reduction of approximately $50 million of resources ($9 million represents labor resources) along the U.S.-Mexican border and $38 million ($11 million represents labor resources) along the U.S.-Canadian border. The opening of the Canadian side of the U.S.-Canadian border by the Motor Vehicle Transportation Act of 1987, which came after Canadian trucks were allowed to enter the U.S. by MCA, caused establishments to locate at the ports of entry. This result is attributed to the effectiveness of anti-cabotage laws stemming from the unilateral deregulation of the border causing increased competition for backhaul loads. It is estimated that $64 million worth of resources ($18 million represents labor resources) located at each of the ports of entry along the border.

It is the effectiveness of the laws against cabotage that prevent the use of these results to predict NAFTA's effects on the infrastructure along the U.S.-Mexican border. One could argue that the final effect of the unilateral deregulation of the U.S.-Canadian border by MCA of 1980 and the MVTA of 1987 will mirror the effects NAFTA will have on the infrastructure along the U.S.-Mexican border. If this is so, the combined effects of the Motor Carrier Act and the Motor Vehicle Transportation Act show a per port of entry net increase of $21.53

million of resources in the form of local trucking and courier service establishments ($5.93 million representing labor resources), and $3.65 million of resources in the form of establishments used to arrange transportation for freight and cargo ($1.63 million representing labor resources) to locate at the border. Thus, it appears that opening both sides of the U.S.-Mexican border will produce a net increase in resources along the border devoted to transborder trucking.

NAFTA was suppose to reduce the barriers for transborder trucking across the U.S.-Mexican border. NAFTA, unlike the combined effects of MCA and MVTA, would enable Mexican and Canadian truckers to partially circumvent the laws against cabotage in the U.S. Along the U.S.-Canadian border, if the rules against cabotage were removed, it is unlikely that the border agents discussed above would be necessary at the ports of entry. The border agents would not be needed to consolidate backhaul loads for Canadian truckers because, once in the U.S., Canadian truckers could perform domestic U.S. pickups and deliveries until a load back to Canada is located. The number of establishments at the ports of entry would be reduced to the levels essential for the normal facilitation of the movement of goods in a free market. After NAFTA unilaterally deregulates the borders, anti-cabotage laws will be weakened which increases the probability of securing backhaul loads in the U.S. A Canadian trucker will be able to transport cargo into the U.S. where he/she will be able to pick up cargo and transport it to destinations in Mexico as well as Canada, whereas before NAFTA the Canadian trucker could only backhaul to Canada. Once in Mexico, the Canadian trucker can pickup freight and transport it into the U.S. The Canadian trucker's movements would be exempt from the anti-cabotage laws because the movement is not performed solely in the U.S. This will effectively decrease the Canadian trucker's probability of an empty haul inside the United States and will weaken the effectiveness of anti-cabotage laws which will reduce the demand for services for freight consolidation at the border.[21] This leaves the question: will the decrease in the demand for interlining services be greater than the increase in the demand for services to fill empty backhauls? Again, this is an empirical question that cannot be answered here. Thus, using the U.S.-Canadian border after MCA and MVTA as a model of the U.S.-Mexican border after NAFTA would produce erroneous predictions.

Table 5-2: U.S. Nominal Tariff Rates by Commodities (1991)

Product	tariff rate	Product	tariff rate
citrus-fruits-juices	23.0	other-wood	8.335
other-fruit	13.0	dairy-products	8.4
sugar-containing-products	10.0	cotton	10.0
vegetables	9.0	automobile	2.5
livestock-meat-cattle	2.0	light-duty-trucks	25.0
poultry	6.4	automobile-parts	3.1
fish	17.5	electronic-products	4.2
cut-flowers	8.0	machine-tools	2.9
rum	13.7	bearings	7.0
wines	6.15	textiles	7.0
beer	1.7	apparel	18.0
rough-wood-products	2.55	pharmaceuticals[a]	3.5
lumber	0	steel-mill-products[a]	4.0
veneer	0	flat-glass[a]	4.8
particle-board	2.0	household-glassware	16.0
fiberboard	3.0	chemicals	4.0
plywood	8.5	industrial-machinery	0.1
builders-joinery	3.75	major-household-appliances[a]	0.8
siding-flooring-molding	3.8		

Source: U.S. International Trade Commission. 1993. Potential Impact on the
U.S. Economy and Selected Industries of the North American Free-Trade
Agreement. USITC Publication. (January).

[a] Effective U.S. rate of duty.

Table 5-3: Parameter Estimates for Equations (5.2) and (5.3)

	U.S.-Canadian Border		U.S.-Mexican Border	
	rportimp	ln(truck)	rportimp	ln(truck)
rportimp	—	0.02715	—	0.0156
		(3.767)		(3.705)
portcomp	—	0.0906	—	0.0038
		(4.009)		(0.700)
pctAG	-6.7444	0.2813	0.0277	0.0062
	(-1.677)	(2.678)	(0.237)	(1.691)
rGDP	0.0426	—	0.0151	—
	(3.292)		(3.070)	
tariff	-2.1928	—	-0.2793	—
	(-0.829)		(-1.131)	
exchgrte	9.7726	—	5.2201	—
	(0.318)		(3.081)	
mca80	—	0.0643	—	0.1947
		(0.571)		(0.546)
brra82	—	—	—	-0.3280
				(-2.256)
mcsa84	—	—	—	-.3233
				(-2.755)
mvta87	—	-0.3129	—	—
		(-2.932)		
Detroit	219.3037	-4.1666	—	—
	(6.053)	(-2.213)		
Ogdensburg	28.3435	-3.2031	—	—
	(0.827)	(-5.368)		
Buffalo	91.9851	-1.8078	—	—
	(2.676)	(-1.581)		
Constant	-27.4885	5.6056	—	—
(Pembina)	(-0.398)	(4.176)		
Laredo	—	—	33.3313	3.4239
			(12.135)	(9.567)

Table 5-3 (continued)

	U.S.-Canadian Border		U.S.-Mexican Border	
	rportimp	ln(truck)	rportimp	ln(truck)
El Paso	—	—	5.6576	-0.8138
			(3.718)	(-1.917)
San Diego	—	—	-1.3769	-1.0435
			(-0.869)	(-10.272)
Constant	—	—	-27.4161	-4.5131
(Nogales)			(-1.577)	(-22.416)
Adj. R-Square	0.9491	0.9942	0.9155	0.9702
No. obs.	57	65	63	58

t-statistics are in parentheses.

Note: The standard error of the coefficients may not be a consistent estimate of the true standard error. The t-statistics in the table are from the Huber regression from the statistical package Stata. Stata does not automatically correct the standard errors in a Huber regression when one of the independent variables is instrumented. However, the adjusted R^2 associated with the regressions used to obtain the instrumental variable for the 2SLS regressions was greater than 90 percent, indicating a good fit. Therefore, the standard error may be smaller than the true standard errors but the difference should not be too much greater.

Table 5-4: Parameter Estimates for Equation (5.1)

	421- Local Trucking and Courier Service		422- Public Warehousing and Storage		473- Arrangement for Transport of Freight	
	U.S.-Can.	U.S.-Mex.	U.S.-Can.	U.S.-Mex.	U.S.-Can.	U.S.-Mex.
truck	0.000516	0.0002826	.00000923	0.000031	0.000057	0.000053
	(1.367)	(4.525)	(1.215)	(2.627)	(4.153)	(3.140)
mca80	-17.2041	-46.40571	-0.8803	0.2174	-2.9502	-0.3004
	(-2.745)	(-3.030)	(-0.749)	(0.090)	(-1.993)	(-0.087)
brra82	—	16.3873	—	-2.2315	—	2.1155
		(2.202)		(-1.724)		(0.880)
mcsa84	—	34.9578	—	1.5033	—	8.089
		(2.649)		(0.859)		(2.920)
mvta87	27.5886	—	1.6688	—	7.0101	—
	(2.464)		(1.264)		(2.132)	
Laredo	—	13.9825	—	0.2398	—	35.0788s
		(3.204)		(0.149)		(6.274)
San Diego	—	153.7567	—	20.273	—	27.6495
		(14.535)		(6.363)		(10.104)
El Paso	—	43.0520	—	8.1343	—	9.2281
		(5.768)		(6.012)		(3.426)
Constant (Nogales)	—	-15.5713	—	0.5912	—	1.9205
		(-3.051)		(0.495)		(1.206)

Table 5-4 (continued)

	421- Local Trucking and Courier Service		422- Public Warehousing and Storage		473- Arrangement for Transport of Freight	
	U.S.-Can.	U.S.-Mex.	U.S.-Can.	U.S.-Mex.	U.S.-Can.	U.S.-Mex.
Detroit	165.953	—	24.6312	—	45.49388	—
	(11.700)		(8.358)		(5.784)	
Buffalo	258.4296	—	8.2975	—	-1.8872	—
	(12.225)		(2.609)		(-0.372)	
Ogdensburg	-1.5189	—	0.9157	—	1.2973	—
	(-0.534)		(1.127)		(1.069)	
Constant (Pembina)	4.7773	—	0.0160	—	-1.5717	—
	(1.602)		(0.182)		(-1.665)	
Adj R square	0.9830	0.9194	0.9578	0.5947	0.9816	0.6329
No. obs.	57	48	56	52	56	50

t-statistics are in parentheses.

Note: The standard error of the coefficients may not be a consistent estimate of the true standard error. The t-statistics in the table are from the Huber regression from the statistical package Stata. Stata does not automatically correct the standard errors in a Huber regression when one of the independent variables is instrumented. However, the adjusted R^2 associated with the regressions used to obtain the instrumental variable for the 2SLS regressions was greater than 90 percent, indicating a good fit. Therefore, the standard error may be smaller than the true standard errors but the difference should not be too much greater.

Table 5-5: U.S. Imports from Mexico by Mode and Commodity

		Mexico		
	STCC/Description	Truck	Total $	% carried by truck
01	Farm Products	2,206,849	2,282,679	97
08	Forest Products	1,580	2,101	75
09	Fresh Fish or other Marine Products	35,762	70,408	51
10	Metallic Ores	19,282	86,773	22
13	Crude Petroleum, Natural Gas, Gasoline	1,345	44,398,333	0
14	Nonmetallic Minerals; except Fuels	31,758	5,862,419	1
19	Ordnance or Accessories	191	325	59
20	Food or Kindred Products	1,392,782	2,198,920	63
21	Tobacco Products	90	6,066	1
22	Textile Products	55,391	82,918	67
23	Apparel	142,893	169,764	84
24	Lumber or Wood Products	448,771	484,994	93
25	Furniture or Fixtures	639,434	749,830	85
26	Pulp, Paper, or Allied Products	85,325	166,612	51
27	Printed Matter	19,339	45,032	43
28	Chemicals or Allied Products	135,843	1,400,087	10
29	Petroleum or Coal Products	141,745	3,433,006	4
30	Rubber or Misc. Plastics	82,858	105,397	79
31	Leather or leather Products	41,116	43,292	95
32	Clay, Concrete, Glass, Stone Products	601,882	3,458,113	17
33	Primary Metal Products	400,549	1,228,482	33
34	Fabricated Metal Products	2,916,886	2,969,153	98
35	Machinery, except Electrical	2,986,296	3,622,035	82
36	Electrical Machinery or Equipment	13,230,594	13,390,454	99
37	Transportation Equipment	128,001	1,367,749	9
38	Instruments or Photographic Goods	158,951	173,685	92
39	Misc. Products of Manufacturing	349,329	367,660	95
40	Waste or Scrap Materials	0	162,393	0
00	Unidentified	562,938	1,009,312	0

Source: U.S. Department of Agriculture. Transportation and Marketing
    Division. 1992. U.S.-Mexico Bilateral Trade: Estimated Modal Shares. By
    Keith A. Klindworth. Table 6. (September): 6.
Note: Estimated volumes, 1991 (short tons).

NOTES

1. James Giermanski and David Neipert note that Mexican registration requirements mandate that only licensed Mexican Customs brokers may process Mexican inward manifest. This may create a potential problem once NAFTA is enacted because it essentially gives Mexican Customs brokers a monopoly in the market for Customs clearing services (House 1996, 291-2; also see Molina and Giermanski 1994, 53).

2. A certificate of registration is required for truck services (International Trade Comm. 1995, 40-2). Brokers and freight forwarders must have a bond, insurance policy, or other type of security approved by the Secretary of Transportation in order to be issued a certificate of registration (Senate 1995, 87). In 1987, transportation property brokers were required to post a $10,000 bond (Senate 1987, 2).

3. SIC 421 are establishments used in transporting freight, SIC 422 are warehousing establishments, and SIC 473 are establishments used to arrange transportation of goods. Refer to the Appendix for more detailed descriptions.

4. Nationwide, transportation property brokerage firms employ a median of 3.0 employees (Brown 1990, 53).

5. The best estimate of the scalar market price for interlining services would be the average revenue of the typical firm in the industry. Since the typical firm's average revenue is $TR/N = PQ/N$, then by substitution $TR/N=P(1/\phi)N/N =(1/\phi P)$, where TR denotes total revenue.

6. Jordan and Burns (1984, 487), report that MCA made it possible for grocery stores in the U.S. to save $165 million by reducing empty backhauls.

7. Four digit SICs are preferred over the three digit SICs, but because of disclosure rules of the Bureau of the Census a sufficient number of observations at the four digit level were not available. In addition, the four digit SICs were redefined in 1988 making some categories unusable for present purposes; however, the change did not affect the three digit codes. For a detailed description of each SIC see appendix.

8. During the writing of this book, U.S. Customs in Washington D.C. relocated. In a telephone conversation, Customs told me that data on the number of inbound trucks at the port level prior to 1982 has been lost in move.

9. I determined dutiable rate though a simple regression: $DUTYRATE = 6.86 MFG + 8.4689 AGL$, where DUTYRATE denotes the nominal ad valorem tariff rates of imports into the U.S. and MFG and AGL are dummy variables taking on the value of one if the commodities are industrial products or agricultural products, respectively, and zero otherwise. This method yields the

sample means, a more accurate measure would weight each observation by the amount of each good imported. The data used in the regression are listed in table 5-2 at the end of this chapter.

10. Each Custom district has one of the above mentioned ports of entry. The number of inbound trucks passing through the ports of entry map quite closely the number of inbound truckers through all the ports of entry along each border. Evidence of this was presented in Chapter 4.

11. For the year 1980, the percent of agricultural exports from Mexico was not available.

12. An alternative measure might be the purchasing price parity foreign currency exchange rate.

13. Data for the number of inbound trucks through the port of San Diego for the year 1978 was not available from the department of Customs.

14. If the Durbin-Watson is greater than d_U (the upper bound of the Durbin-Watson statistic) then there is evidence of no first-order serial correlation. If it is less than d_U then either there is evidence of serial correlation or no conclusion can be drawn. To be on the safe side, unless there is evidence of no first-order serial correlation, the Cochrane-Orcutt procedure was used to correct for the possibility serial correlation. The Cochrane-Orcutt procedure was perform using an estimate of the first order autocorrelation coefficient obtained by the Theil-Nagar method (Theil and Nagar 1961).

15. Huber's procedure is the same as White's correction. The Huber procedure corrects the diagonal elements of the variance-covariance matrix by using the squared residuals of the regression to estimate the heteroskedastic unknown variances.

16. This functional form provides direct estimates of the percentage change in the number of inbound trucks based on changes in the independent variables.

17. The trucking network between the U.S. and Canada began developing after the Motor Carrier Act of 1980. Canadian carriers began their networks at population centers nearest to the U.S.-Canadian border and continued branching deeper into the U.S. Canadian Less-than-Truckload firms located hubs near the ports of entry and employed U.S. truckers to make U.S.-domestic delivery and pickups. This gave Canadian transborder truckers an international hub where freight could be consolidated for backhauls to Canada. This reduced Canadian carriers' problem of empty hauls caused by the anti-cabotage laws. (Chow and McRae 1990, 9-11). Also, because of higher transportation rates in Canada, many Canadian small businesses bypassed the use of Canadian carriers by opting to rent trucks and privately transport their goods to the border and

interline with lower-cost U.S. truckers. (Chow 1991, 152) This encouraged U.S. trucking firms to establish hubs near the ports of entry along the international border.

18. In an investigation of the U.S.-Canadian trucking industry, Ex Parte No. MC-157, the investigator showed that in 1980 in the Less-Than-Truckload sector 13.2 percent of international shipments were single-lined (carried by one trucker) while 86.8 percent were inter-lined (two truckers exchanged cargo). For the Truckload sector, 22.1 percent were single-lined, while 77.9 percent were inter-lined. Ninety-three percent of the truckload freight and seventy-nine percent of the LTL freight transported between the U.S. and Canada originated from the U.S. (House 1983, 145).

19. In a prepared statement before the House Public Works and Transportation Committee: Surface Transportation Subcommittee, by Philip W. Haseltine, Deputy Assistant Secretary for Policy and International Affairs of the U.S. Department of Transportation, notes that Mexico once attempted reciprocity concerning truck entry in 1955. In 1955, Mexico signed the Ruiz Cortines Decree that was supposed to allow U.S. truckers into the border zone along Mexican side of the border; however, this decree has never been upheld by Mexican authorities. There are some cases in which truckers have entered Mexico, but generally U.S. truckers are denied entry into the Mexican transborder market (House 1987, 42).

20. There were no metropolitan listings that closely represent Pembina, ND, and Ogdensburg, NY.

21. Anti-cabotage laws have been reduced recently. U.S. Customs ruled that foreign vehicles may make pickups within the U.S. so long as the movement is incidental to the trucks leaving the U.S. (Binkley 1997, 41; Binkley 1998, 38).

CHAPTER 6

Conclusion

Transborder trucking between U.S., Canada, and Mexico has encountered, over a fairly recent time period, an array of regulations that affect the direct-lining of cargo between the three countries. Attention paid to transborder trucking has increased since the Motor Carrier Act of 1980 opened the U.S. borders to foreign truck entry. Prior to this act, the U.S.-Mexican and U.S.-Canadian borders were unilaterally closed by protective trucking regulations put in place by the three nations. Two years after the MCA of 1980 opened the U.S. side of the border, regulations intensified that eventually closed the southern border to Mexican truckers. The 1982 Bus Regulatory Reform Act partially closed the U.S.-Mexican border to Mexican trucks who carried ICC regulated cargo, then two years later, the Motor Carrier Safety Act completely closed the border to Mexican truckers through heightened safety regulations. Since 1980, the U.S.-Canadian border has enjoyed increased liberalization of truck entry regulations. Seven years after the Motor Carrier Safety Act was put into law, Canada opened the Canadian side of the U.S.-Canadian border to U.S. truckers. This was made possible by the Motor Vehicle Transportation Act of 1987. The Act was the final action necessary to make the northern border unilaterally free of truck entry regulations. To this day, the U.S.-Canadian border is open to single-line movements of transborder shipments. However, the U.S.-Mexican border has remained closed to transborder trucks since 1984 and all shipments must be interlined at border crossings.

Trucking in Mexico is quite different than trucking in Canada. Canada has a well developed trucking industry, similar to the U.S., with well developed trucking networks. The Canadian trucking industry is comparable to the U.S. industry in many aspects, including excellent roads and highways. Mexico, on the other hand, does not have well developed trucking networks. The less-than-truckload industry, fully developed in the U.S. and Canada, is in its infancy in Mexico. The Mexican road system is antiquated and poorly engineered for trucking, but through privatization, the quality of the roads is improving.

Much of the information about Mexican transborder truckers being unskilled and drive unsafe tractor trailers cannot be trusted. More often than not, data on transborder trucking are collected at border crossings by either survey or inspection (see U.S. General Accounting Office, 1996). The data are then erroneously assumed to be random samples of the transborder trucking industry. In fact, the data are representative samples of a specialized subset of the transborder trucking industry, namely the drayage industry. Because of barriers to entry at the border, trucking companies often enlist the services of drayage firms to transport their cargo across the international border to be interlined with foreign transborder truckers on the other side. The drayage firms' equipment is often older tractors and/or trailers used only to make the short hauls across the border. In many cases, the drayage trucks do not meet Mexican or U.S. highway safety standards. These vehicles do not represent the typical vehicles of the transborder trucking industry, and these drayage firms would be the first eliminated once the border is open to single-line shipments. Though Mexican trucks are reported to be older than their U.S. counterparts, Mexican trucking firms have strong economic incentive to ensure that their trucks are well maintained and safe. To stay in business and maximize profit in a competitive environment, trucking firms must convince their customers that their shipments will arrive on time and free of damage. Timely and reliable delivery requires well maintained equipment.

Though Mexican employees working in the transportation industry are paid roughly twenty percent less than their U.S. counterparts, transborder truckers are highly paid in the Mexican trucking industry. It has been reported that Mexican transborder truckers require superior training and are compensated with higher pay.

Entry regulations have affected foreign truckload sizes carried into the U.S. When the U.S. opened its borders in 1980 by the Motor Carrier Act, which allowed foreign truckers to single-line shipments into the U.S., interlining at the border was no longer necessary. This allowed foreign truckers to avoid the fixed costs associated with interlining shipments at the border. The lower costs allowed the truckers to carry lighter loads into the U.S. The MCA of 1980 reduced Mexican truckers' fixed cost to the point where load sizes decreased by 19.7 percent. Inbound Canadian trucks crossing the U.S.-Canadian border experienced an 18.9 percent decrease in load sizes. When the U.S. closed the U.S.-Mexican border by the Bus Regulatory Reform Act and the Motor Carrier Safety Act, transborder movement costs increased by the amount of the fixed cost of interlining. As a result, Mexican truckload sizes increased to their former levels, which is roughly 20 percent higher than the period of open access to the U.S. made possible by the MCA. Once unilateral deregulation is achieved and the two sides of the border are open, while anti-cabotage laws are enforced, foreign truckers will likely carry heavier loads on fronthauls into the U.S. compared to backhauls out of the U.S. The reason is that deregulation of transborder entry regulations increases competition for international cargo. If anti-cabotage laws remain intact, foreign truckers will be geographically restricted in finding backhauls once inside the U.S. Domestic truckers thus have an advantage over foreign carriers in securing international cargo in the U.S. Foreign truckers will incorporate the lower probability of obtaining full backhauls into their decision making and carry heavier loads on their fronthauls to make up the difference. Thus, the higher revenues from the fronthauls offset the expected losses from the backhauls on transborder movements into the U.S. Data used in this study are not rich enough to confirm this theory, and it is left as an area for future research.

Not only are load sizes affected by regulations, but the number of inbound trucks entering the U.S. and the infrastructure along the borders also are affected by transborder truck entry regulations. The results from this study show that the two regulations that closed the southern border to Mexican truckers, the Bus Regulatory Reform Act of 1982 and the Motor Carrier Safety Act of 1984, reduced the number of inbound trucks per port of entry by roughly 32 percent. Also the Motor Vehicle Transportation Act of 1987, which lifted the barriers to entry on the Canadian side of the U.S.-Canadian border and allowed unilateral entry by both nations' trucks, decreased the number of inbound trucks by roughly 31 percent. Interestingly enough, with all the congressional attention concerning the alleged mass entry of Mexican truckers into the U.S. after the passing of the Motor Carrier Act of

1980, empirically the number of inbound trucks did not increase significantly during this time.[1]

The border infrastructure and the fluctuations in the number of establishments used to facilitate the interlining of transborder shipments offer a means of measuring the amount of resources allocated toward the ports of entry as a result of changes in transborder regulations. Holding the number of inbound trucks constant and looking only at four of the busiest ports of entry along each border, it is estimated that opening the U.S. side of the international borders by the 1980 Motor Carrier Act caused 17.2 and 46.4 local trucking and courier service establishments per port of entry to move away from the U.S.-Canadian and U.S.-Mexican borders, respectively. Establishments involved in the arrangement for the transport of freight and cargo decreased by 2.9 establishments per port of entry along the U.S.-Canadian border. The establishment changes are direct results of deregulation along the borders. The exodus of local trucking and courier service establishments represents estimates as high as $35.62 million and $49.93 million worth of resources that moved away from each port of entry along the U.S.-Canadian and U.S.-Mexican border, respectively. The exit of establishments involved in the arrangement for transport of freight and cargo represents a resource allocation as high as $2.65 million per port of entry along the U.S.-Canadian border.

The Bus Regulatory Reform Act of 1982, which partially closed the U.S.-Mexican border by restricting ICC operating authorities, caused an estimated increase of 16.39 local trucking and courier service establishments per port of entry to locate along the U.S.-Mexican border. This represents a resource allocation to the border totaling $17.63 million per port of entry. The Motor Carrier Safety Act of 1984, that essentially closed the U.S.-Mexican border to all Mexican truckers though heighten safety regulations, caused an estimated 34.90 local trucking and courier service establishments per port of entry to locate along the U.S.-Mexican border. This is an estimated $37.60 million of resources to locate at each port of entry. The MCSA also caused a per port of entry estimate of 8.09 establishments involved in arranging for transportation for freight and cargo to locate at the border. This represents an estimated $17.80 million worth of resources to locate at each port of entry along the border upon its closure.

By closing the border to foreign truckers, resources are allocated in a way that consumers lose while a smaller segment of the economy is made better off. Truck entry regulations divert resources away from productive activities in the U.S. and locates them at the border. The interlining of cargo is an unnecessary operation that causes the price of imports and exports to increase. This is a disadvantage for consumers but a benefit for the agents who perform interlining services already located at the border. However, this is a short-run result. The economic agents at the border can capture the price increases in the form of higher profits. The higher profits last only for a short time because with low barriers to entry in the interlining service industry, any above normal profits will quickly attract firms to the border to provide interlining services. The entry of interlining service establishments at the border will increase the supply of interlining services, forcing interlining service prices to fall. As prices fall, entry into the industry slows to a stop when the real interlining service prices fall to levels where the border agents earn normal rates of return. The agents that locate along the border come from other areas in the country, reducing the amount of resources available to provide services in the domestic market. The fewer resources create a long-run disadvantage for consumers. With fewer resources to produce domestic goods and services, prices will increase. Thus, from an economic welfare vantage point, by closing the border, not only do consumers pay higher prices on foreign goods, but consumers also lose by paying higher domestic prices.

The winners from closing the border are domestic truckers and the communities along the border. Truckers benefit by less competition from foreign truckers. With fewer foreign truckers with whom to compete, U.S. truckers can charge higher rates and earn economic rents. It is cited in the transport literature that unionized trucking benefited the most from restricting domestic entry (Annable 1973; Moore 1978; Kim 1984; Rose 1985; Hirsch and Macpherson 1998). The harm of deregulation in 1980 came in the form of lower hourly wages for unionized trucker (Rose 1987; Hirsch 1988). James Peoples (1996) found that in the unionized for-hire trucking industry wages fell by 5.63 percent (there was no apparent affect on non-union for-hire wages) and hours per week worked fell throughout the industry. Thus, unionized trucking has strong incentive to lobby to keep the border closed. For the communities along the border, although interlining establishments earn zero economic profit in the long run, their numbers are increased, which benefits labor along the border. Therefore, it can be construed that transborder truck entry regulations transfers welfare from domestic consumers to truckers (possibly exclusively to unionized truckers) and the communities along the border.

The most interesting and probably the most important result for today's policymakers is the combined effects of the Motor Carrier Act and the Motor Vehicle Transportation Act. Once NAFTA is fully implemented, the U.S.-Mexican border will be open for unilateral entry by U.S. and Mexican truckers. The only model we have of unilateral deregulation of truck entry barriers for the U.S. is the U.S.-Canadian border after both the Motor Carrier Act and the Motor Vehicle Transportation Act. It is estimated that the Motor Vehicle Transportation Act caused 27.6 local trucking and courier service establishments and 7.0 establishments involved in the arrangement of transportation for freight and cargo to locate around each port of entry along the U.S.-Canadian border. This represents a per port of entry resource allocation totaling $46.47 million for local trucking and courier service establishments and $3.55 million dollars for establishments used in arranging transportation for freight and cargo. This increase is attributed to the fact that cabotage prohibits both U.S. and Canadian truckers from making pickups and deliveries within the other's country. By not being able to perform cabotage, truckers find it difficult to locate backhaul loads to carry out of the other's country. Establishments locate along the border to consolidate shipments for truckers to backhaul to their home country. Thus, anti-cabotage laws, by increasing the number of establishments at the border, are also distorting devices that divert productive resources away from the markets unnecessarily. Combining the effects of the Motor Carrier Act and the Motor Vehicle Transportation Act results in an increase totaling $17.50 million for local trucking and courier service establishments and $2.05 million dollars for establishments that arrange transportation for freight and cargo per ports of entry. To summarize, deregulating the border by MCA had a decreasing effect on the number of establishments located at the ports of entry, while anti-cabotage laws after MVTA had a dominate increasing effect along the border. Thus, using the opening of U.S.-Canadian border as a model for the U.S.-Mexican border after NAFTA, it appears that unilaterally deregulating the U.S.-Mexican border will divert resources toward the border.

NAFTA has at least one consideration that makes it unique from the deregulation of the U.S.-Canadian border. This consideration, as such, warrants caution in formulating policies base on the above results. To avoid prosecution from anti-cabotage laws, a foreign trucker with the authority to transport freight into the U.S. may not transport and deliver freight between any two points within the U.S. The trucker may make pickups, but once freight is picked up in the U.S., the foreign trucker must deliver the freight outside the country without a delivery along the way.[2] Once the U.S.-Mexican border is opened, Mexican truckers may be able to partially circumvent the anti-cabotage laws. Once a Mexican trucker is in the U.S., it has two destinations to transport freight: Mexico and Canada. This is an alternative Canadian truckers did not have after the U.S.-Canadian border was deregulated. Being able to transport freight to Canada, a Mexican trucker under NAFTA will expect a higher probability of full backhauls in the U.S. than Canadian truckers expected after MCA and MVTA. This increases the distance Mexican truckers can haul into the U.S. and reduces the effects of the anti-cabotage laws. Using the U.S.-Canadian border and the combined effects of MCA and MVTA as a model for trucking after NAFTA would exaggerate its impact on the infrastructure along the border. This over-estimation must be considered when formulating policies concerning the regulation of transborder trucking.

Further research to reveal the effects of regulating transborder trucking is needed. The importance of this research increases as NAFTA comes closer to fruition. Policymakers are currently showing outward signs of hesitancy to lift regulations on foreign truck entry into the U.S. One can only imagine the reason for their trepidation. Reasons are given that Mexican trucks are safety hazards, but there is little credible evidence that this is the case. Is it that policymakers are being conscientious but ignorant of the effects that their policy actions have on the allocation resources? This is possible given that little has been written on transborder trucking in the economics literature. Or is it that policymakers are being opportunistic and appeasing special interest groups?[3] Whatever the reason for prohibiting transborder trucking, further research is warranted to increase our knowledge of the effects that these regulations have on the allocation of resources.

NOTES

1. In other research (Jones forthcoming), the Motor Carrier Act of 1980 was found to significantly increase the number of inbound trucks.

2. Formally, the interpretation and enforcement of the anti-cabotage law was that once a pickup is made in the U.S., a foreign trucker must traverse the same route from which it entered the U.S.

3. The reluctance to deregulate U.S. domestic trucking prior to the MCA of 1980 has been attributed to policymakers being captured by the industry that they were regulating (Stigler 1971).

Definition of Standard Industrial Codes

The three SIC's of interest are SIC 421—Local Trucking and SIC 422,—Courier Service, Public Warehousing and Storage, SIC 473—Arrangement of Transportation of Freight and Cargo, (SIC Manual, 1987, pp. 270—281).

The standard industrial code (SIC) 421, trucking and courier services, incorporates many different forms of trucking. Included under this SIC are local trucking with and without storage, general trucking (except local), and courier services (except by air). Local trucking without storage consists of trucks generally operating within commercial zones. Examples of such trucking establishments are trucks used for carting, draying, and general local transport with or without storage such as furniture moving, garbage and refuse hauling, trucks used for logging, baggage transfer, local contract bulk mail carriers, local rental trucks with drivers, and local agriculture hauling (including hauling of live animals). General trucking (except local) are firms primarily providing "over-the-road" trucking services which would include some storage services. Generally, they operate outside of municipalities. Included in this category would be long-distance hauling. Local trucking with storage are trucking companies that primarily operate within municipalities and have storage as part of their business. They include local furniture moving, household goods moving, and generally all local trucking involved with storage. Courier services (except by air) are firms that primarily deliver individual letters, or parcels, but not including the United States Postal Service. Packages delivered by couriers are usually under 100 pounds.

153

Examples of these kinds of trucking companies are courier services, letter delivery, and private mail delivery.

Public warehousing and storage, SIC 422, consists of farm product warehousing and storage. Firms in this category are responsible for storage of agricultural goods that do not involve cold storage. Examples include bean and grain elevator for storage only, cotton compresses, wool and mohair, and tobacco warehouses. Refrigerated warehousing and storage are establishments engaged in cold storage. They primarily store perishable food goods. They may own or rent out space, or offer services involving preparing or packaging for cold storage. Examples of these types of establishments would be cold or freezer warehousing of cheese or other food items. General warehousing and storage firms involve typical warehousing like self-storage or miniwarehouses. Another category of warehousing that falls under the SIC 422 is special warehousing and storage. These establishments usually store special products. Examples of these include warehousing for dead storage of automobiles, fur for trade, furniture, household goods, goods in foreign trade zones, textiles, and whiskey. They are also engaged in storage for hire involving lumber terminals, oil and gasoline, petroleum, and chemical bulk stations and terminals.

The category SIC 473, arrangements of transportation of freight and cargo, contains the agents engaging in or providing shipping information for arrangement of freight and cargo to be transported for a fee. Examples of these agents are transportation brokers of cargo, freight rate auditors, tariff consultants, customhouse brokers, Custom clearance of freight, domestic and foreign freight forwarders, and shipping documents preparation.

In 1987 the Department of Commerce redefined the standard industrial codes, and in 1988, the *County Business Patterns* adhered to the redefinition. Data for years prior to 1988 were changed to correspond to post 1988 definitions. Some four digit SICs were affected. The SIC 4212 - local trucking without storage, 4213 - trucking (except local), 4214 - local trucking with storage, 4215 - courier services (except by air) were all subsumed into 421 - trucking and courier services (except by air) after 1988. Categories 471 - freight forwarding, and 4723 - freight transportation arrangement were combined into 473, now called freight transportation arrangement.

Bibliography

Adrangi, Bahram, Garland Chow, and Kambiz Raffiee. 1995. Analysis of the Deregulation of the US Trucking Industry. *Journal of Transport Economics and Policy*. (September): 233-246.

Allen, Benjamin, and Boguslaw Liberadzki. 1987. A Comparative Study of the Trucking Industries of the United States of America and Poland: Part B. An Overview of the Trucking Industry in the United States of America. working paper. University of Illinois at Urbana-Champaign, no. 1361 (May):1-40.

Allen, Bruce W. and Dong Liu. 1995. Service Quality and Motor Carrier Costs: An Empirical Analysis. *The Review of Economics and Statistics* 77 (3):499-509.

Annable, James E. Jr. 1973. The ICC, the IBT, and the Cartelization of the American Trucking Industry. *Quarterly Review of Economics and Business* 13 (2):33-47.

Austin, John S. and Rosenbaum. 1990. The Determinants of Entry and Exit Rates into U.S. Manufacturing Industries. *Review of Industrial Organization* 5(2) (summer):211-223.

Averch, Harvey and Leland L. Johnson. 1962. Behavior of the Firm Under Regulatory Constraint. *American Economic Review* 52(5):1052-1069.

Barnekov, Christopher C. 1987. The Track Record. *Regulation*, no. 1: 19-27.

Barnes, David, 1997. No Border Opening Date: U.S. Cities Safety Concerns, Mexico Points to Discrimination, Cabotage and 53-foot Trailers. *Traffic World* 252(11). 15 December: 14

Bayliss, Brian T. 1986. The Structure of the Road Haulage Industry in the United Kingdom, and Optimum Scale. *Journal of Transport Economics and Policy* 20(2) (May):153-172.

155

Belzer, Michael H. 1995. Collective Bargaining After Deregulation: Do the Teamsters Still Count. *Industrial and Labor Review* 48(4) (July): 636-655.

Bennett, Randall W. and Kenneth D. Boyer. 1990. Inverse Price/Quality Tradeoffs in the Regulated Airline Industry. *Journal of Transportation* 29(1) (January):35-47.

Best, Annie. 1993. Freight Forwarders and Custom Brokers Help Handle Cross-Border Transport. *Traffic World* 235(1). 5 July: 36-38.

Binkley, Alex. 1998. U.S. Frees Reins on Canadian Truckers: Customs Proposal Would Allow for Incidental Movements, More Efficient Cross-Border Trade. *Traffic World* 254(10). 8 June: 38.

———. 1997. Canadian Truckers Get Better U.S. Access: U.S. Customs Changes Cabotage Rules' INS Still Must Rule on Canadian Drivers Working in U.S. *Traffic World.* 3 November: 41.

Bowman, Robert J. 1991. Adios Mordida. *World Trade* 4(7) (November):88-96.

Boyer, Kenneth D. 1993. Deregulation of the Trucking Sector: Specialization, Concentration, Entry, and Financial Distress. *Southern Economic Journal* 59(3): 481-495.

Braeutigam, Ronald R. and Roger G. Noll. 1984. The Regulation of Surface Freight Transportation: The Welfare Effects Revisited. *The Review of Economics and Statistics* 66(1):80-87.

Brown, Stewart. 1995. The Effects of Property Broker Authority on Motor Carrier Transportation Capacity. *Logistics and Transportation Review* 31(2) (June):161-178.

Brown, Terrence A. 1990. Size and Operation Characteristics of Property Brokers. *Transportation Journal* 29(4) (summer):52-57.

———. 1984. Freight Brokers and General Commodity Trucking. *Transportation Journal* 24(2) (winter): 4-19.

Buckley, Tom. 1994. Mexico's Long-Awaited Trucking Weight Regulations Meet with Little Enthusiasm on Both Sides of Border. *Traffic World* 237(12). 21 March: 22-24.

Bureau of the Census. U.S. Department of Commerce. Economics and Statistics Administration. 1992. *Census of the Transportation, Communications, and Utilities: Geographic Area Series: Summary.*

———. U.S. Foreign Trade Division. 1989-93. Imports for Consumption by U.S. Customs District of Entry. *Merchandise Trade: Selected Highlights.* FT920.

————. U.S. Foreign Trade Division. 1977-88. Imports of Consumption - U.S. Coastal Area and Customs District (Customs Value Basis). *Highlights of U.S. Export and Import Trade*. FT990.

Burke, Jack. 1994. Uncertainty, Surprises Still Dominate Cross-Border Transport With Mexico. *Traffic World* 237(12). 21 March: 20-21.

Button, Kenneth, and David Pitfield. 1991. *Transport Deregulation: An International Movement*, St. Martin's Press, New York: 141-176.

Carroll, Paul B. 1995. Speedier U.S.-Mexico Traffic is Sought: Coalition's Plan is Aimed at Better Technology, Easier Rules for Trucks. *Wall Street Journal*. 19 September: A19.

Carroll, Paul B., and Craig Torres. 1995. Optimism Remains for Mexican Economy: Despite Peso's Weakness, Business Leaders See Growth Resuming Soon. *Wall Street Journal*. 13 November: A11.

Central Intelligent Agency. 1997. Mexico. *CIA World Factbook*. http://www.odci.gov/cia/publications/factbook/country-frame.html.

Chapman, Stephen. 1977. Too Much: The ICC and the Truckers. *Washington Monthly*. (December): 36.

Childs, William R. 1985. *Trucking and the Public Interest: The Emergence of Federal Regulation 1914-1940*. The University of Tennessee Press.

Chow, Garland and James J. McRae. 1990. Non-Tariff Barriers and the Structure of the U.S.- Canadian (Transborder) Trucking Industry. *Transportation Journal* 30(2) (Winter): 4-21.

Chow, Garland. 1995. North American Trucking Policy. *International Business, Trade and Finance Working Paper*. Ref. no. 95-036. University of British Columbia.

————. 1991. US and Canadian trucking policy. In *Transportation Deregulation an International Movement*, edited by Kenneth Button and David Pitfield. St. Martin's Press: 141-176.

————. 1983. How Much Longer Can We Live with Regulation of Canada's Trucking Industry. *The Canadian Business Review* 10(1): 45-52.

Christensen, Lawrit R. and John H. Huston. 1987. A Reexamination of the Cost Structure for Specialized Motor Carriers. *Logistics and Transportation Review* 23(4) (December).

Clayton, A. and J. Sem. 1985. Regulatory Issues in Transborder Trucking: A Case Study Referencing Trucking Between Manitoba and Minnesota. 20th Annual Meeting, proceedings. *Canadian Transportation Research Forum*. (May): 263-292.

Council of Economic Advisers. 1994. *Economic Report of the President*: 230-270.

Crum, Michael, R. 1985. The Expanded Role of Motor Freight Brokers in the Wake of Regulatory Reform. *Transportation Journal*. (summer): 5-15.

Daughety, Andrew F. and Forrest D. Nelson. 1988. An Econometric Analysis of Changes in the Cost and Production Structure of the Trucking Industry, 1953-1982. *The Review of Economics and Statistics* 70(1): 67-75.

Davis, Grant M. 1981. Economic Essays on Issues in the Motor Carrier Industry. *Motor Carrier Economics, Regulation, and Operation*. University Press of America: 9-14.

De Santis, Solange. 1998. U.S. Traps Canadians in a One-Size-Fits-All Border-Control Policy. *Wall Street Journal*. 4 June: A13.

Delaney, Robert V. 1987. The Disunited States: A Country in Search of an Efficient Transportation Policy. *Cato institute: Policy Analysis*. no. 84, 10 March.

Dempsey, Paul Steven. 1991. Running On Empty: Trucking Deregulation and Economic Theory. *Administrative Law Review* 43(253) (spring): 253-319.

Doyle, Gary T. 1997. Not All's Well with NAFTA Trucking. *Distribution* 40(7) (June).

DRI/McGraw-Hill; Standard & Poor's; U.S. Department of Commerce/ International Trade Administration. 1998. Chapter 43 in *U.S. Industry & Trade Outlook*.

Economist Intelligence Unit. 1992-93. *Mexico, Country Profile*. 40 Duke Street, London W1A 1DW.

Ellison, Anthony P. 1984. Regulatory Reform in Canada: A Different Ball Game: Trucking. *Regulatory Regimes in Conflict: Problems of Regulation in a Continental Perspective*. edited by Fred Thompson. University Press of America, inc.: 119-136.

Emerson, Carol J., Curtis M. Grimm, and Thomas M. Corsi. 1991. The Advantage of Size in the U.S. Trucking Industry: An Application of the Survivor Technique. *Transportation Research From: Proceedings of the 33rd Annual Meeting*: 333-342.

Farver, Deena. 1993. No Room in the Warehouse. *Business Mexico* 3(7) (July): 6.

Fawcett, Stanley E., and David B. Vellenga. 1992. Transportation Characteristics and Performance in Maquiladora Operations. *Transportation Journal* 31(4) (summer): 5-16.

Felton, John Richard and Dale G. Anderson. 1989. *Regulation and Deregulation of the Motor Carrier Industry*. Iowa State University Press.

Finger, J. M. and A. J. Yeats. 1976. Effective Protection by Transportation Costs and Tariffs: A Comparison of Magnitudes. *Quarterly Journal of Economics* 90: 167-176.

Gagné, Robert. 1990. On the Relevant Elasticity Estimates of Cost Structure Analyses of the Trucking Industry. *The Review of Economics and Statistics*. February: 160-164.

Gee, J. M. A. 1985. Competitive Pricing for a Spatial Industry. *Oxford Economic Papers* 37: 466-485.

Giermanski, Jim, Kelly S. Kirkland, Eduardo Martinez, David M. Neipert and Tom Tetzel. 1990. *U.S. Trucking in Mexico: A Free-Trade Issue*. Texas Center for Border Economic and Enterprise Development.

Giordano, James N. 1989. A Trucker's Dilemma: Managerial Behavior Under an Operating-Ratio Standard. *Managerial and Decision Economics* 10(2): 241-251.

Gooley, Toby B. 1993[a]. Shipping to Canada. *Traffic Management* 32(4) (April): 90A-92A.

———. 1993[b]. Shipping to Mexico. *Traffic Management* 32(4) (April): 93A-94A.

———. 1991. U.S. Carriers Head South of the Border. *Traffic Management* 30(11) (November): 47-49.

Gorys, Julius M. L. 1987. Ontario-United States Border Truck Movements. *Transportation Quarterly* 41(3) (July): 347-364.

Greenberger, Robert S. 1995. Mexican Trucks Face U.S. Delay on Freer Travel. *Wall Street Journal*. 19 December: A2.

Grimm, Curtis M. and Robert Windle. 1997. Regulation and Deregulation in Surface Freight, Airlines and Telecommunications. In *Regulatory Reform and Labor Markets*. edited by James Peoples. Kluwer Academic Publishers.

Grimm, Curtis M., Thomas M. Corsi, and Judith L. Jarrell. 1990. U.S. Motor Carrier Cost Structure Under Deregulation. *Logistics and Transportation Review* 25(3): 231-249.

Grunwald, Joseph, 1990/91. Opportunity Missed: Mexico and Maquiladores. *The Brookings Review*, winter: 44-48.

Hall, Kevin. 1993. U.S. Customs Brokers Seek Antitrust Probe of Alleged Violations by Mexican Rivals. *Traffic World* 235(1). 5 July: 34-36.

Hansen, Nales, 1986. *Across Boundaries Transborder Interaction in Comparative Perspective*. Texas Western Press. Edited by Qscar J. Martinez: 31-44.

Harmatuck, Donald J. 1981. A Motor Carrier Joint Cost Function: A Flexible Functional Form with Activity Prices. *Journal of Transport Economics and Policy* 15(2) (May):135-152.

Hearings: Canadian Truckers Cite Opportunities for U.S. Truckers in Canadian Market. 1982. *Traffic World* 190(3), 19 April: 73-74.

Hirsch, Barry T. 1988. Trucking Regulation, Unionization, and Labor Earnings: 1973-85. *Journal of Human Resources* 23(3) (summer): 296-319.

Hirsch, Barry T. and David A. Macpherson. 1997. Earnings and Employment in Trucking: Deregulating a Naturally Competitive Industry. In *Regulatory Reform and Labor Markets*. edited by James Peoples. Kluwer Academic Publishers.

Hoyle, Brian S. 1993. Transport in Canada: Patterns Issues and Trends. *Journal of Transport Geography* 1(3) (September): 147-149.

ICC Approves 25% Rate Reduction by Eastern Railroads on Some Iron and Steel Products, Effective May 1. 1950. *Wall Street Journal* 135(94), 22 April: 3.

International Monetary Fund. 1994. *International Financial Statistics Yearbook* XLVII: 516-517.

Interstate Commerce Commission. 1992. *The U.S. Motor Carrier Industry Long After Deregulation: A Report by the Office of Economics Interstate Commerce Commission* (March).

———. 1981. *The Effect of Regulatory Reform on the Trucking Industry: Structure, Conduct, and Performance.* (June).

———. 1976. *Ex Parte No. MC-37 (Sub-No. 26): Commercial Zones and Terminal Areas.* Washington, D.C.

James, Robert and Janice Hughes. 1993. Knowing Pact Would Die Today, pro-NAFTA Lobby Mobilizes for Tomorrow. *Traffic World.* 5 July: 25-27.

James, Robert. 1994. DOT: Border Ready for NAFTA, but Not Roads Leading To It. *Traffic World.* 17 January: 21.

Joint U.S.-Mexican Group Meets, but Little Advance Made on Truck Differences. 1982. *Traffic World.* 6 September: 63.

Jones, John T. forthcoming. The Effects of Transborder Trucking Regulations on Inbound Trucks and the Trucking Infrastructure. *The Journal of Transport Economics and Policy.*

Jordan, William C. and Lawrence D. Burns. 1984. Truck Backhauling on Two Terminal Networks. *Transportation Research-B* 18B(6): 487-503.

Joy, Stewart. 1964. Unregulated Road Haulage: The Australian Experience. *Oxford Economic Papers* 16(2) (July): 275-285.

Kafoglis, Milton. 1977. Valuable Operating Rights in a "Competitive" Industry: A Paradox of Regulated Trucking. *Regulation*. September/October: 27-32.

Kahn, Alfred E. 1988. *The Economics of Regulation: Principles and Institutions. vol's.* 1 & 2, The MIT Press Cambridge, Massachusetts London, England.

Keeler, Theodore E. 1989. Deregulation and Scale Economies in the U.S. Trucking Industry: An Econometric Extension of the Survivor Principle. *Journal of Law and Economics* 32 (October): 229-253.

Kim, Moshe. 1984. The Beneficiaries of Trucking Regulation, Revisited. *Journal of Law and Economics* 27 (April): 227-241.

Kling, Robert W. 1990. Deregulation and Structural Changes in the LTL Motor Freight Industry. *Transportation Journal* (spring): 47-53.

———. 1988. Trucking Deregulation: Evolution of a New Power Structure. *Journal of Economic Issues* 22(4) (December): 1201-1211.

Koenker, Roger. 1977. Optimal Scale and the Size Distribution of American Trucking Firms. *Journal of Transportation Economics and Policy* 11: 54-67.

Kraas, Alexander. 1993. The Impact of the US Motor Carrier Act 1980 on Road Safety in California: An Econometric Policy Evaluation. *Logistics and Transportation Review* 29(2): 179-192.

Landero, Alejandro Diaz. 1990. An Economic Appraisal of the Deregulation Process In The Mexican Transport Market. *Journal of the Transportation Research Forum* 31: 101-108.

Lasky, Julio. 1995. Logistics Technology in Mexico. *Canadian Customs Guide*. Livingston Trade Service Inc. (June).

Mabley, Robert E. and Walter D. Strack. 1982. Deregulation-A Green Light for Trucking Efficiency. *Regulation* (July/August): 37-42.

Madras, Mark L. 1989. The Regulating of Transportation Intermediaries. *Transportation Practitioners Journal* 56: 132-150.

Magee, Stephen P.; William A Brock, and Leslie Young. 1989. *Black Hole Tariffs and Endogenous Policy Theory: Political Economy in General Equilibrium*, Cambridge University Press.

Major Railroads Showed a Deficit of $9 Million in February . . . 1950. *Wall Street Journal* 135 (8): 6 April: 1.

Mallick, Rajiv and Elias G. Carayannis. 1994. Regional Economic Convergence in Mexico: An Analysis by Industry. *Growth and Change* 25 (summer): 325-334.

Maltz, Arnold, James R. Giermanski and David Molina. 1996. The U.S.-Mexico Cross-Border Freight Market: Prospects for Mexican Truckers. *Transportation Journal* (fall): 5-19.

Maltz, Arnold, Linda Riley, and Kevin Boberg. 1993. Purchasing Logistics Services in a Transborder Situation: Logistics Outsourcing in US-Mexico Co-production. *International Journal of Physical Distribution and Logistics* 23(8): 46-54.

Matthews, Anna Wilde. 1998. On the Borderline: Nafta Reality Check: Trucks, Trains, Ships Face Costly Delays. *Wall Street Journal*. 3 June: A1 & A10.

McCallum, John, 1995. National Borders Matter: Canadian-U.S. Regional Trade Patterns. *American Economic Review* 3(85) (June): 615-623.

McCray, John P. 1993. Truck Transportation Opportunities and the North American Free Trade Agreement. Presented to the 1993 American Trucking Associations Management Conference. 1 November.

McCray, John P. and James E. Groff. 1990. Maquiladora Purchasing Patterns: Opportunities and Obstacles for U.S. and Mexican Border Firms. *Southwest Journal of Business and Economics* 7(2) (fall): 31-38.

McMullen, Star B. and Hiroshi Tanaka. 1995. An Econometric Analysis of Differences Between Motor Carriers: Implications for Market Structure. *Quarterly Journal of Business and Economics* 34(4) (autumn): 16-28.

McMullen, Starr B. 1987. The Impact of Regulatory Reform on U.S. Motor Carrier Costs. *Journal of Transport Economics and Policy*. 21(2): 307-319.

McMullen, Starr B. and Linda R. Stanley. 1988. The Impact of Deregulation on the Production Structure of the Motor Carrier Industry. *Economic Inquiry* 26 (April): 299-316.

Melvin, James. 1985. Tariffs and Domestic Transportation Costs. *Canadian Journal of Economics* 18(2) (May): 237-257.

Mercer Management Consulting Co. 1992. Railroad Implications of Free Trade with Mexico (July).

Meyer, John R., Merton J. Peck, John Stenason and Charles Zwick. 1959. *The Economics of Competition in the Transportation Industries*. Harvard University Press, Cambridge, Massachusetts: 348-353.

Molina, David and James R. Giermanski. 1994. *Linking or Isolating Economies? A Look at Trucking Along the Texas-Mexico Border*. U.S. Mexican Policy Report No. 6. Lyndon B. Johnson School of Public Affairs. The University of Texas at Austin.

Moore, Thomas Gale. 1983. Rail and Truck Reform-the Record So far. *Regulation*, Nov./Dec.: 33-42.

————. 1982. Deregulation and Re-regulation of Transportation. Policy Analysis. Cato Institute. 8 July.

————. 1978. The Beneficiaries of Trucking Regulation. *Journal of Law and Economics* 21(2): 327-343.

————. 1972. *Freight Transportation Regulations: Surface Freight, and the Interstate Commerce Commission.* Washington American Enterprise Institute for Public Policy Research.

Muller, E. J. 1992. Forwarders vs. Brokers. *Distribution* 91(6), (June): 38-43

Nelson, James C. 1936. The Motor Carrier Act of 1935. *Journal of Political Economy* 44(4) (August): 464-504.

Nicholson, Howard W. 1958. Motor Carrier Costs and Minimum Rate Regulation. *Quarterly Journal of Economics* 72(1) (February): 139-155.

Noll, Roger G. 1988. Regulation After Reagan. *Regulation.* no. 3: 13-20.

Oum, Tae Hoon. 1979. A Cross Sectional Study of Freight Transport Demand and Rail-Truck Competition in Canada. *The Bell Journal of Economics* 10(2) (autumn): 463-482.

Peoples, James. 1996. Trucking Deregulation and Labour earnings in the USA: a Re-examination. *Applied Economics* 28(7): 865-874.

Plamer, John P. 1988. The Canadian Trucking Industry. chapter 4 in *An Economic Analysis of Canada's Ground Transportation Sector.* The Fraser Institute: 59-126.

————. 1973. A Further Analysis of Provincial Trucking Regulation. *The Bell Journal of Economics and Management Science* 4(2) (Autumn): 655-664.

Prentice, Barry E., and Marvin D. Hildebrand. 1989. Transborder Trucking: Institutional Barriers to Canada-U.S. Trade of Agricultural Goods. *Journal of the Transportation Research Forum* 29: 65-72.

President. 1994. NAFTA Transportation Provision. 103th Cong., 2nd sess. (7 October): H. Doc. 103-323.

Pustay, Michael. 1989. Deregulation and the US Trucking Industry. In *The Age of Regulatory Reform.* Edited by Kenneth Button and Dennis Swann. Clarendon Press. Oxford: 237-256.

————. 1978. The Social Costs of Monopoly and Regulation: An Empirical Evaluation. *Southern Economic Journal* 45(2) (October): 583-591.

Rakowski, James P. 1988-89. The Market Failure in LTL Trucking: What Hath Deregulation Brought? *Transportation Practitioners Journal* 56: 33-43.

Robyn, Dorothy. 1987. *Braking the Special Interests: Trucking Deregulation and the Politics of Policy Reform.* The University of Chicago Press, Chicago and London.

Rose, Nancy L. 1987. Labor Rent Sharing and Regulation: Evidence from the Trucking Industry. *Journal of Political Economy* 95(6): 1146-1178.

———. 1985. The Incidence of Regulatory Rents in the Motor Carrier Industry. *Rand Journal of Economics* 16(3) (autumn): 299-318.

Rousslang, Donald, and Theodore To. 1993. Domestic Trade and Transportation Costs as Barriers to International Trade. *Canadian Journal of Economics* 26(1) (February): 208-221.

Russell, Stephen. 1998. Doing Business in Mexico: Staying the Course Pays Dividends. *International Business* 11(2): 16-18.

Schiller, Dane. 1991. Hauling South. *Business Mexico* 1(8) (October): 18-20.

Schulz, John D. 1998[a]. Big Getting Bigger: Consolidation Trend Predicted to Race Amid Booming Projections in truckload," *Traffic World* 235(1). 9 March: 15.

———. 1998[b]. Recovery Indeed: National, Regional LTL Carriers Enjoy Fiscal Fruits of Cost-Saving Moves, Improved Pricing, Efficiencies. *Traffic World* 253(6). 9 February: 15-17.

———. 1993. U.S. Truckers Eager to Capitalize on Fast-Growing Mexico Market. *Traffic World* 235(10). 5 July: 27-30.

Skorochod, Peter, and Rob P. Bergevin. 1984. Issues in Transportation/Distribution for the Small/New Exporter. Annual Meeting. *Canadian Transportation Research Forum*. issue 19.

Slack, Brian. 1993[a]. Pawns in the Game: Ports in a Global Transportation System. *Growth and Change* 24 (fall): 579-588.

———. 1993[b]. The Impacts of Deregulation and the US-Canada Free Trade Agreement on Canadian Transportation Modes. *Journal of Transport Geography* 1(3) (September): 150-155.

———. 1990. Intermodal Transportation in North America and the Development of Inland Load Centers. *Professional Geographer* 42(1): 72-83.

Sloss, James. 1970. Regulation of Motor Freight Transportation: A Quantitative Evaluation of Policy. *Bell Journal of Economics* 1(32):327-366.

Smith, Brian R. 1993. Contractual Governance in Trucking: Maislin v. Primary Steel and the Undercharge Crisis. *The American Economist* 37(1) (spring): 56-63.

Snow, John W. 1977. The Problem of Motor Carrier Regulation and The Ford Administration's Proposal for Reform. In *Regulation of Entry and Pricing in Truck Transportation*. edited by Paul W. MacAvoy, and John Snow, American Enterprise Institute for Public Policy Research, Washington D.C.: 3-43.

Snow, John W. and Stephen P. Sobotka. 1977. Certificate Values. In *Regulation of Entry and Pricing in Truck Transportation.* edited by Paul W. MacAvoy, and John Snow, American Enterprise Institute for Public Policy Research, Washington D.C.: 153-156.

South, Robert B. 1990. Transnational "Maquiladora" Location. *Annals of the Association of American Geographer* 80(4): 549-570.

Spychalski, John C. 1997. Developments in Transport Policy: From ICC to STB: Continuing Vestiges of US Surface Transport Regulations. *Journal of Transport Economics and Policy* (January): 131-136.

Stanbury, W.T. 1984. Trucking Wars. in Appendix 1. *Regulatory Regimes in Conflict: Problems of Regulation in a Continental Perspective.* edited by Fred Thomas, University Press of America, inc.: 133-136.

Standard & Poor's 1997. Transportation: Commerce. *Industry Survey* 2(I-Z) 17 July: 1-35.

Statistics Canada. Transportation Division Surface and Marine Transport Section. 1996. *Trucking in Canada.* catalogue no. 53-222-XPB.

Steinberg, Carol. 1993. The Road to Mexico. *World Trade* 6(6) (June): 92-98.

Stewart, Joy. 1964. Unregulated Road Haulage: The Australian Experience. *Oxford Economic Papers* 16(2) (July): 275-285.

Stigler, George J. 1971. The Theory of Economic Regulation. *Bell Journal of Economics* 2 (spring): 3-21.

———. 1968. *The Organization of Industry.* The University of Chicago Press, Chicago.

Stoner, Seigh. 1989. U.S.-Canadian Cross-Border Traffic Continues to Undergo Radical Change. *Traffic World* 220(5). 30 October: 20-21.

Tabburri, Rosanna. 1995. Crossing U.S.-Canada Border is Likely to Be Simplified for Frequent Travelers. *Wall Street Journal.* 27 November: A14.

Taske, Paul, Samuel Best, and Michael Mintrom. 1995. *Deregulating Freight Transportation: Delivering the Goods.* Washington D.C.: The AEI Press.

Tausz, Andrew. 1989. Free Trade's Impact on Transportation. *Chilton's Distribution* 88 (May): 30-33.

Taylor, Phillips H. and Miles H. Sonstegaard. 1993. Two Measures of the Motor Carrier Transportation Cost of Commodities. *Arkansas Business and Economic Review* 25(3): 1-17.

Theil and Nagar. 1961. Testing the Independence of Regression Disturbances. *Journal of the American Statistical Association* 56: 793-806.

Thomas, Janet M. and Scott J. Callan. 1992ᵃ. An Analysis of Production Cost Inefficiency. *Review of Industrial Organization* 7(2): 203-226.

————. 1992[b]. Cost Analysis of Specialized Motor Carriers: An Investigation of Aggregation and Specification Bias. *Logistics and Transportation Review* 28(3): 217-230.

U.S. Department of Transportation. Bureau of Transportation Statistics. 1994. Transborder and International Freight Value by Mode. *North American Transportation: Statistics on Canadian, Mexican, & United States Transportation.* Table 16. (May):16.

U.S. Department of Agriculture. Transportation and Marketing Division. 1992. *U.S.-Mexico Bilateral Trade: Estimated Modal Shares.* By Keith A. Klindworth. Table 6. (September): 6.

U.S. Department of Commerce. 1993. Chapter 40 in *U.S. industrial Outlook.* (January): 9-14.

U.S. Department of Commerce. Economics and Statistics Administration. 1977-94. *County Business Patterns.*

U.S. Department of Commerce. International Trade Administration. 1992. U.S. Export to Mexico, 1987-91: State Export Profile. *Exports to Mexico: A State-By-State Overview 1987-1991.* (July).

U.S. Department of Labor. 1990. Industrial Effects of a Free Trade Agreement Between Mexico and the US. 15 September. PB91-110627.

U.S. Department of States. 1993. Country Reports on Economic Policy and Trade Practices, Mexico Economic Policy and Trade Practices. 28 July.

U.S. Department of States. 1994. Economic Policy and Trade Practices: Mexico. *Country Reports on Economic Policy and Trade Practices.* 27 August.

U.S. Department of Transportation. 1990. *The Impact of State Economic Regulation of Motor Carriage on Intrastate and Interstate Commerce: Final Report: DOT-T-90-12* (May).

U.S. Department of Transportation. 1993. *Intermodel Surface Transportation Efficiency Act: Section 1089 and Section 6015: Assessment of Border Crossings and Transpiration Corridors for North American Trade, Report to Congress.*

U.S. Federal Trade Commission. Bureau of Economics. 1988. *Deregulation in the Trucking Industry.* by Diane S. Owen. May.

U.S. General Accounting Office 1978. *ICC's Expansion of Unregulated Motor Carrier Commercial Zones has had Little or No Effect on Carriers and Shipper.* Report to the Congress of United States. GA0 B-1887797, CED-78-124. microfiche.

U.S. General Accounting Office. 1993. *Mexican Trucking Wages.* microfiche. RCED-94-78R; B-255696, 12 November: 2-10.

U.S. General Accounting Office. *Commercial Trucking: Safety and Infrastructure Issues Under the North American Free Trade Agreement.* GAO/RCED-96-61 (February).

U.S. General Accounting Office. Committee on Finance. 1991. *Survey of U.S. Border Infrastructure Needs: Report to the Chairman.* GA 1.13 NSIAD-92-56.

U.S. House. 1983. Subcommittee on Surface Transportation of the Committee on Public Works and Transportation. *Foreign Motor Carrier Operations.* 98th Cong., 7 October: report 98-31.

U.S. House. 1986. Subcommittee on Surface Transportation of the Committee on Public Works and Transportation. *Deregulation of Surface Freight Forwarders: S.1124 - To Amend Title 49, United States Code, to Reduce Regulation of Surface Freight Forwarders, and for Other Purposes.* 99th Cong. 2nd sess. 18 June. report 99-49.

U.S. House. 1987. Subcommittee on Surface Transportation of the Committee on Public Works and Transportation. *International Motor Carrier Relations between the United States and Mexico and Regulatory Exemptions.* 100th Cong. 1st sess. 26 March. report 100-9.

U.S. House. 1995. *ICC Termination Act of 1995.* 104th Cong. 1st sess. 18 December. report 104-422.

U.S. House. 1996. Committee on Transportation and Infrastructure. Subcommittee on Surface Transportation. *Reauthorization of ISTEA: North American Free Trade Agreement, Border Infrastructure and Motor Carrier Safety, Laredo and Pharr TX.* 104 Cong. 2nd sess. 8 & 9 August. report 104-80.

U.S. International Trade Administration. 1993. Mexico-Economic and Trade Policy - ETP920300. *Market Research Reports.* CD-Rom. 28 July.

U.S. International Trade Commission. 1995. *Harmonized Tariff Schedule of the United States (1995): Annotated for Statistical Reporting Purposes.* USITC Publication 2831: 40-42.

U.S. Senate. 1987. Committee on Commerce, Science, and Transportation. *Transportation Property Brokers.* 100th Cong. 1st sess. 13 November. report 100-494.

U.S. Senate. 1991. Committee on Commerce, Science, and Transportation. *Interstate Commerce Commission Freight Motor Carrier Oversight.* 102th Cong. 1st. sess. 19 September. report 102-516.

U.S. Senate. 1993. Committee on Commerce, Science, and Transportation. *Surface Transportation Implications of NAFTA: Hearing before the*

Committee on Commerce, Science, and Transportation. 103th Cong. 1st sess. 4 May. report 103-157.

United Nations. various years. *International Trade Statistics yearbook: Trade by Country.* vol.1.

Valdes, Rafael J. and Michael R. Crum. 1994. U.S. Motor Carrier Perspective on Trucking in Mexico. *Transportation Journal* 33(4) (spring): 5-20.

Warf, Barney, and Joseph Cox. 1993. The U.S.-Canada Free Trade Agreement and Commodity Transportation Services among U.S. States. *Growth and Change* 24 (summer): 341-364.

Waters, W. G. 1970. Transportation Costs, Tariffs, and the Pattern of Industrial Protection. *American Economic Review* 60(5) (December): 1013-1020.

Weiner, Paul. 1971. The Use of the Operating-Ratio-Revisited. *Public Utility Fortnightly* 88. 5 August: 33-42.

Willig, Robert D. and William J. Baumol. 1987. Using Competition as a Guide. *Regulation* no. 1: 28-35.

Wilson, Wesley W. and Richard Beilock. 1993. Market Access Decisions in Regulated and Unregulated Markets: The Continuing Cost of Interstate Motor Carrier Regulation. *Working paper Series.* No 137. University of Oregon. Department of Economics.

Winston, Clifford, Thomas M. Corsi, Curtis M. Grimm, and Carol A. Evans. 1990. *The Economic Effect of Surface Freight Deregulation.* Washington, D.C.: The Brooking Institute.

Winston, Clifford. 1981. A Disaggregate Model of the Demand for Intercity Freight Transportation. *Econometrica* 49(4) (July): 981-1006.

Ying, John S. 1990[a]. Regulatory Reform and Technical Change: New Evidence of Scale Economies in Trucking. *Southern Economic Journal* 77(2) (April): 996-1009.

Ying, John S. 1990[b]. The Inefficiency of Regulating a Competitive industry: Productivity Gains in Trucking Following Reform. *The Review of Economics and Statistics* 72(2) (May): 191-201.

Ying, John S., and Theodore E. Keeler. 1991. Pricing in a Deregulated Environment: the Motor Carrier Experience. *Rand Journal of Economics* 22(2) (summer): 264-273.

Zurier, Steven. 1991. Distribution's Mexican Connection. *Industrial Distribution* 80(1) (January): 26–30.

Index

For Product Safety Concerns and Information please contact our EU representative GPSR@taylorandfrancis.com Taylor & Francis Verlag GmbH, Kaufingerstraße 24, 80331 München, Germany

Printed and bound by CPI Group (UK) Ltd, Croydon, CR0 4YY

08/05/2025

01864340-0001